*Welcome to Sunday*

# Welcome to Sunday

*An Introduction
to Worship in the
Episcopal Church*

*Christopher L. Webber*

MOREHOUSE PUBLISHING
*A Continuum imprint*
HARRISBURG • LONDON • NEW YORK

Copyright ©2003 by Christopher L. Webber

Morehouse Publishing
P.O. Box 1321
Harrisburg, PA 17105

*Morehouse Publishing is a division of Continuum.*

*Printed in the United States of America*

*Cover design by Brenda Klinger*

Library of Congress Cataloging-in-Publication Data

Webber, Christopher.
  Welcome to Sunday: an introduction to worship in the Episcopal Church / Christopher L. Webber.
     p. cm.
  ISBN 0-8192-1915-0 (pbk.)
  1. Public worship—Episcopal Church. 2. Episcopal Church—Liturgy. I. Title.
  BX5940 .W43 2003
  264'.03—dc21                                    2002010567

# Contents

# Introduction:
# What Is Worship?

Some people come into an Episcopal church for the first time and are thrilled with the worship they discover; others come in and are baffled. But no matter what their instinctive response, they often find themselves in the same boat as the old Scottish sea captain who wandered into an Episcopal church one Sunday. Since he was unfamiliar with the service, he later told friends he had survived by "putting down my anchor and rising and falling with the tide." Like the sea captain, many worshipers in the Episcopal Church, some of them longtime members, are still somewhat mystified by the service they take part in every week. They have never really begun the journey to unlock its full richness and meaning. A successful sea captain understands the stars and tides, and plans a trip to take advantage of them. It is always better to understand as fully as possible, so that our spiritual journey will have greater direction and depth. This book explores the history and traditions of worship in the Episcopal Church, so that both lifelong members and new arrivals will learn not only to survive, but participate with new understanding, and be enriched by the experience.

The last book of the Bible, the Book of Revelation, portrays heaven itself as one great outpouring of worship. An old

Scottish catechism, which the sea captain might have memorized, says that the chief end of human life is "to worship God and enjoy him for ever." If that is true, and we were, indeed, made for worship and are intended to offer worship eternally, it makes good sense to invest time and thought in learning to do it better now.

But what do we mean by worship? Many church notice boards speak of "Worship Services," but what happens at the advertised hour may be different in every parish. In some churches, "worship" consists of hearing a sermon, singing hymns, listening to prayers, and putting money in the collection plate; in others it is an outpouring of gospel hymns and speaking in tongues; in still others, it means watching a priest at a distant altar. For worshipers themselves, the experience varies as well: it may be primarily intellectual, or emotional, or mostly a matter of habit. But whatever worship looks like or feels like, it is only a means to an end: to create and nourish a relationship with God with other Christians. Worship has to do with relationships, and Christians believe that life itself is a matter of relationships: we are who we are because of the people to whom we are related. If we are related to no one, we die. If we are related to God, we live. Therefore we worship.

Human relationships vary widely: some are vital and emotional, some primarily intellectual, some casual and occasional. A few special ones remain a constant part of our lives. Our relationship with God can fit into those same categories. As a relationship between husband and wife would be unsatisfactory if it were simply intellectual or purely emotional, so a relationship with God is unsatisfactory if it is one sided. Any relationship is certainly better than nothing, but growth in our relationship with God is essential to our spiritual life. St. Augustine is often quoted as having said, "You have made us for yourself, O Lord, and our hearts are restless until they find

rest in you." Worship, in other words, is not an optional relationship but one vital to our health and well-being. We were
made for worship. Without it, we are likely to be plagued by
the nagging feeling that something is missing from our lives.
Yet how many of us put worship at the center of our lives or
make any significant effort to grow in our understanding of
worship until we know at the center of our being how much
our lives depend on worship, how much they are enriched by
it?

Let's admit right away that thinking about worship as a
matter of relationships is not always comfortable for Americans. We hear people say, "I have my own religion" or "I can
worship God in my own way." But if that were true, and worship were primarily a solitary pursuit, it would be fundamentally different from almost every other aspect of human life.
Human beings can't live alone. Primitive people knew that:
they had to work together to ensure the tribe's survival. Scholars tell us that the Hebrew language of the Bible has no word
for an individual body, only for the flesh of which we are all
made. It seemed obvious to the Hebrews that life is shared,
that our whole existence is bound up with others. But somehow we like to imagine that we can "get along" by ourselves, as
if the complexities of modern society had reduced our need for
each other. The fact is, modern technology has made us more
dependent on each other than ever, and at the same time has
created a rising tide of dissatisfaction. Although we are linked
with each other more closely than ever by jet planes and e-
mail, many people feel alienated, that their lives are incomplete
and unsatisfying. Some imagine that the solution is to find
ways to drop out or get away from it all. What we need instead
is to offer our lives to God in worship so that the pressures and
tensions are transformed. The "global village" we have discovered needs a soul.

Christians speak of being part of the "Body of Christ." St. Paul says we are "members of Christ" as truly as hands and feet and head are part of a body and depend on each other. Coming together for worship, then, is a very natural way of acting out the connection that is already deeply part of our humanity. We are "members one of another," sharing a common life and uniting in common worship. The book Episcopalians use is called a "Book of *Common* Prayer" for good reason.

Worship may be intended to prepare us for heaven, but we need to admit right away that worship in the Episcopal Church is not always heaven on earth. The perfection of heavenly worship can be wrinkled and torn by human foibles and idiosyncrasies. Perhaps the preacher has an odd habit of addressing his remarks to a spot somewhere in the rafters, or one of the acolytes is constantly fiddling with the rope around her vestment, or the organist's hymnal falls on the keyboard shattering a solemn moment, or someone in a nearby pew whispers loudly to a friend during silent prayer. In a baseball game, the errors are recorded for all to see on the scoreboard, but in most human activities, we accept them as part of the human package. In spite of the distractions that are part of life, most of us know how to get our jobs done and still attend to those we love. So, too, in worship we express our love for God and realize God's love for us in an imperfect world, but we will do it better and with less concern for the interruptions as we grow in understanding and experience. Worship, like anything worthwhile, rewards the effort we make. The great saints of the past and faithful Christians we know today can assure us that a deeper relationship with God is well worth the time spent in worship.

Is it really possible, then, to have "our own religion" or our own way of worship? Is there nothing to be learned from the great saints of the past or the more experienced Christians around us? A recent article about children and computers reported that boys tend to ignore instructions and "just punch buttons until something works." Maybe that's what some of us do when it comes to worship. But computers are only toys we create for our use; God, on the other hand, created us and remains beyond the comprehension of the greatest scholars or most deeply committed saints. There is always more to learn, more growth that's possible. This book is designed to lay the groundwork for that learning and growth. If it succeeds, you will be eager to move further still in the endless journey toward the God of life.

# Where and When

## OUTSIDE THE BUILDING

Let's begin our study of worship on the sidewalk outside the church. Stay in your comfortable chair if you like and just picture in your mind the nearest Episcopal church. It may be a gothic building like a small English cathedral, a simple New England meeting house of white-painted wood, or something very modern. Despite all the architectural possibilities, you will almost certainly know an Episcopal church to be a church by one unmistakable sign: a Christian cross on the steeple, wall, or signboard. Of course, many other churches use the cross as well. Is there anything that distinguishes an Episcopal church from any other kind of Christian church? Not necessarily. New England Episcopal churches are more often built of stone, while the buildings of the United Churches of Christ are more often made of white-painted wood, but some Episcopal churches in New England are also wooden and painted white. Nationwide, an Episcopal church is more likely than others to be of stone and use pointed gothic arches, but there are far too many exceptions to make any guidelines possible. Christians, after all, have much in common and increasingly

1

tend to express their faith in similar ways.

Does the church have a tower or spire? Some churches have both, and they make a statement. The white spires of New England churches stand out above the trees as a focal point in the landscape. Whole towns have been built around these landmarks, making them not only the spiritual centers, but also the geographic centers of their communities. The spires point upward, drawing our eyes up and reminding us to look beyond the material concerns of daily life. Churches are here to help us do that. Often the spire is eight-sided: seven sides signify that God made the world in seven days, as recorded in Genesis; the eighth side symbolizes Jesus' resurrection. Traditionally, Christians have viewed the resurrection as the beginning of a new world, an eighth day, an opening to an eternal day. An eight-sided spire points the way to that eternity. Sometimes an eight-sided spire rises from a four-sided tower, symbolizing the "four corners of the earth" that the church draws us from, toward the everlasting day of heaven. There are sermons to be heard from a church without our even going inside!

Still outside, think about the direction in which the church faces. Church builders in America often have little choice about how to site a church: there is a plot of land available and a street on one side. The door must be on the street side and the altar at the other end. But where there is a choice, Episcopal churches normally are built to face east with an entrance at the west end. Why? Because the sun rises in the east, and the first Christians expected Jesus to come again in glory with the rising of the sun. Therefore they built their churches with the altar at the east end so the congregation would be facing east to see Jesus' coming. Whatever way the church actually faces, the altar end of the church is, as a result, called the "east end," and the entrance is usually located in what is called the "west end."

If a church has been built the other way around, this can be very confusing! But knowing the building traditions within the Episcopal Church helps us to understand this terminology, and again, it preaches a sermon without words.

Now, let's look at the door. Church doors are usually bigger than the doors of houses or even stores. Sometimes several doors all lead into the same entrance area. Churches are usually designed with access in mind. They are built to be entered; their ample doors open wide to be welcoming. Often, too, church doors are painted red. Some say church doors have traditionally been painted red for the same reason that barns are: red paint was cheap and durable. Maybe so, but a red door also makes a statement: it draws attention to the entrance. No one should have difficulty finding a church door.

## INSIDE THE BUILDING

Now, step inside (you may have to leave your chair!) and you will usually find yourself in a sort of *vestibule* (or *narthex*), a place to make the transition from the world outside to the worship space further in. Here leaflets with information about the church may be displayed on tables or racks. Perhaps there's a bulletin board with notices of church events. On Sundays ushers or greeters are almost always on hand to welcome you and give you a bulletin with details of upcoming services as well as church activities. Both the literature and the people are there to provide a welcome and to answer questions.

Beyond the vestibule is the space used for worship. What, after all, is a church building for? But worship can take various forms, and the arrangements inside reflect different priorities. One definition of a church building often used in the Episcopal Church is "an altar with a roof over it." Some churches are exactly that. In tropical areas, sometimes churches consist simply of an altar, a roof, and seating, with only the most minimal walls to reduce outside noise. In most Episcopal churches, the altar is clearly the focal point, whether it is against a wall at one end or at the head of the central aisle. It can also be in the center of the worship space with seating on all sides. But not all Christian churches are altar-centered. Some churches think of preaching as primary, and the altar, if there is one, may be a small, seldom-used table.

The location of the altar reflects changing viewpoints on worship. A generation ago, almost all altars were against the far wall, and somewhat distant from worshipers; today they are often much closer to where people sit. The older pattern reflects an understanding of God as a Creator beyond human comprehension; the newer pattern reflects an understanding of God as one who draws near to us in love. Both understandings are true, but there is no way to express both in the same building. In a world where we often feel dominated by distant and hostile forces, the knowledge that God comes near to us in love seems more important.

Even church windows make a statement and contribute to our worship. Some are filled with stained glass reflecting the glory of God and the lives of God's saints, while others, especially in rural areas, are made of clear glass to let us see the beauty of God's world around us. The building and furnishings of a church are intended to speak to us. Episcopal churches especially use color and symbolism to facilitate worship. God is the Creator of all things, and all things can speak to us of God's majesty and God's love.

THE ALTAR

The *altar,* or Lord's *table,* is the focal point in most Episcopal churches. Those two terms—*altar* and *table*—are both commonly used, and each word indicates a different way of looking at what happens there. Here again, both viewpoints are valid. Those who use the term *altar* are those who stress the sacrificial death of Christ for us. He is "the Lamb of God who takes away the sins of the world" (John 1:29) The altar reminds us of sacrifice and is often made of stone and covered with elaborate vestments. It is thought of not only as a place of sacrifice but as being itself the body of Christ. That is why altars are often covered for most of the year, but are stripped on Good Friday, as Jesus' body was.

The altar may also be thought of as the Holy Table, the place where Jesus fed his disciples at the Last Supper, and where he feeds us still today. If this aspect of our worship is stressed, the Lord's table may be made of wood and covered only with a white cloth. Since both ways of understanding the altar/table are important, it would be ideal if we could make an altar/Lord's table of wood/stone. But human minds and tools cannot represent all aspects of God's truth at once. We can only hold on to those aspects that have most meaning for us, at the same time trying to appreciate the insights that others value.

During the service a plate and cup (called the *paten* and *chalice*) are placed on the altar. Candles and vases of flowers may also adorn the altar, or these may be placed on shelves behind the altar. Separating the altar from the rest of the church, an altar rail may be in place, where people may kneel to receive communion. But today, people often stand surrounding the altar to receive communion, or line up and process to the place or places where as clergy and assistants stand, head of the aisle or elsewhere, dispensing communion to those in line.

THE PULPIT

Just as the altar, or Lord's table, cannot express both of its symbolic meanings simultaneously, so the church itself cannot easily have two centers, though perhaps it should. In some periods of church history the pulpit has been the central piece of church furniture, and it still is in some churches, especially those that stress preaching and downplay the sacraments. Sometimes a priest will preach from the aisle, but the pulpit is designed to lift up God's word and give visible dignity and importance to the preaching of that word. As a practical matter, it simply makes it easier to see and hear the preacher. A few Episcopal churches, dating from colonial days, may have a high pulpit in the center. Today most pulpits are located to one side. With today's electronic equipment and less formal society, pulpits in modern churches are often smaller and simpler. In some churches the Bible is read from the pulpit, but more often the Bible is placed on a separate reading desk or lectern, and the appointed passages of Scripture are read from there.

THE FONT

The one other important piece of church furniture is a font. The font (the word is related to the word *fountain*) is usually an eight-sided structure holding a bowl that is filled with water when baptisms take place. Traditionally, fonts are placed near a church door because it is through baptism in the font that we enter the Christian church and become members. In some churches, however, fonts are placed at the front so that it is easier for people to see what is happening there. Why is the font eight-sided? For the same reason as the spire: it is at the font that we become "heirs of eternal life" and begin the life of the new eighth day by sharing in Jesus' resurrection.

SEATING

The largest part of the space inside the church is used for seating the congregation. Usually there are long benches called *pews* where people sit side by side with friends and strangers, but some churches have chairs that are more easily moved, providing greater flexibility. It may be a surprise to learn that pews are a relatively modern invention. Until long after the sixteenth-century reformation, churches had seating only for those who needed it due to age or disability. Most people stood or knelt to take part in services. As sermons became longer, however, nearly everyone began to feel the need for seating, and some individuals began to install pews for their families. The first pews had high sides and doors that isolated people from each other. It has been argued that pews were invented by dissenters, and that they were designed specifically to protect people from clergy intent on making them kneel or bow. Whether that is true or not, they certainly separated families and individuals from each other. Recently, in more peaceful and democratic times, pews have become lower and less divisive. But they still tend to make church members feel like spectators rather than participants. Some churches now encourage people to stand rather than to kneel, and to come forward, out of the pews, and stand around the altar during at least the second part of the service. Sitting, after all, is very passive, but the liturgy is active. Standing and kneeling are more active and involving postures.

Most of the pews or chairs are placed in the part of the church called the *nave,* a word related to "navy" and used because Christians traditionally have thought of the church as a ship designed to carry them from this world to the next. The area in front of the nave is called the *chancel,* and may include seating for a choir, as well as the space around the altar. The altar area is usually called the *sanctuary,* a word meaning a holy place set aside for sacred use. Some churches also contain smaller spaces called *chapels,* which may be used for weekday services.

## SUNDAYS

There was a time when Sundays were different from any other day of the week. Stores were closed, factories stopped, and people who worked a six-day week were freed to spend one day in worship. Both getting ready for church and getting to church took longer then because dress was more formal, and transportation slower. The whole pace of life was slower. Services were not limited to an hour as they often are now; pulpits sometimes held an hour glass to keep the sermon in bounds, but many churches felt no need of even that limit. And, of course, the sermon was only part of the service. And the morning service was not the only church event. People often returned to church in the afternoon for Bible study or a late afternoon service. After all, what else was there to do? There was no television or radio, no shopping mall, no professional sports to watch. In the Puritan tradition, no one was allowed to play games on Sunday, either.

Although the Puritans significantly influenced American history, their customs were never the norm for many other Christians. The Puritans left England, in part at least, because the government refused to prohibit Maypole dances and other such harmless recreation on the Lord's Day. Episcopalians come from a tradition that favors a more balanced approach. Worship must be central, but the Fourth Commandment calls only for rest, not for worship. The fourth of the Ten Commandments tells us to "keep holy the Sabbath day." The Sabbath is the seventh day, or Saturday, and was established to provide a rhythm of rest and work. The Bible says that God created the world in six days and rested on the seventh day; therefore God's people were to observe the same order in their lives. Logically, the day of rest then became the time for worship because people were freed from the daily routines of their work. Jews still observe the seventh day as their day of worship.

For Christians, however, the resurrection of Jesus from the dead created a new world, so they thought it best to worship on a new day, the first day. As we have said, what they initially referred to as the eighth day, we now call Sunday. Every Sunday is first of all a celebration of the resurrection. Even in Lent, Sundays are days of celebration. We have documents from the very first centuries of the church's life that tell how Christians came together on "the day of the Sun" to give thanks to God for the gift of life.

In those first years of the church's existence, Christianity was illegal and Sundays were days of work like any other. Christians came together for worship at daybreak, before the work day began. In recent American history, when the country's business stopped on Sundays, an eleven o'clock service was customary, not only for Episcopalians, but most other Christians as well. By the twentieth century, most Episcopal churches had added an eight o'clock or early-hour service for people who wanted communion each week or who wanted to get an early start on the day. Then, in the last half of the twentieth century, as social patterns changed and an increasingly secular society made Sundays more hectic, most churches replaced the late morning service with one in mid-morning, at ten o'clock or thereabouts. Still more recently, a Saturday evening service has become popular. The biblical day begins at sundown, so Saturday evening is the beginning of the new week. Nowadays, Saturday evenings are often more peaceful than Sundays. A congregation can gather for a service, a potluck meal, and a program without the conflicting pressures of Sunday mornings.

One of the great gifts Episcopalians inherit in the Book of Common Prayer is a pattern of daily worship. The English reformers hoped to preserve a pattern of prayer similar to those of the monasteries, but simplified those prayers so that all

Christians could pray together daily and hear God's word. The services of Morning and Evening Prayer were created for this purpose. There is no reason to limit worship to Sundays alone. If heaven is a place where worship is the primary and constant joy of God's people, we can begin to get into the rhythm here and now. Sunday and weekday worship can and should provide a framework for the whole of life, and all our time, every day.

## QUESTIONS FOR FURTHER
## THOUGHT AND DISCUSSION

1.  Do you agree with the modern view that having altars closer to where people sit, reflecting the knowledge of God's nearness, might be more helpful than the older pattern of having the altar distant from worshipers? Why or why not?

2.  Do you think of the altar as a symbol of Jesus' sacrifice or do you see it more as a table, representing the Last Supper? How did you come to view it as you do?

3.  The author describes the changes in the way people have kept the Sabbath over time. How do you, personally, keep the Sabbath? Is that different than when you were a child? How so? How do you think the Sabbath will be kept in the future, say twenty years from now?

# Who: Ministry

## THE MINISTRY OF THE LAITY

One of the unique characteristics of the Christian faith is the belief that every member is called to ministry. Priesthood in Judaism was inherited, but at baptism all Christians become members of the body of Christ and, therefore, are given a share in his ministry. The New Testament says we are "a royal priesthood" (1 Peter 2:9). The first Christians understood they were sharing in a ministry simply by saying "Amen" to the Prayer of Thanksgiving over the bread and the wine. But they also understood that ministry involved more than coming together for worship: it involved all the church's members all the time. Most of us understand that the ordained clergy are always on call. We may not be as clear about the fact that we are all involved in ministry seven days a week, twenty-four hours a day. We can't stop being who we are just because the church service is over.

When we study the New Testament, we see how the church recognizes the different gifts from the Holy Spirit, and how important it is to use those gifts appropriately. Some, St. Paul wrote, are called to be apostles, others prophets, and still others have gifts as teachers or healers. Some are called to assist while others have gifts for leadership. He compared the church to a body in which the various members' feet and hands, ears and eyes, work together for the good of the whole. He reminded Christians that everyone is important, even those who may seem least significant to us.

On the other hand, in an orderly system, not everyone can or should do everything. To be sure that gifts are properly used, the church developed a pattern of designated ministries. Some, called *bishops* (or *overseers*) were appointed to carry on the apostles' ministry of leadership; others, called *presbyters* (which means *elders*) or *priests* (a shortened form of the same word) were designated to lead local congregations. Still others were set apart for an assisting ministry and became known as *deacons*. Other ministries, less central to the organizational structure of the church, were less formally recognized.

Unfortunately, human beings have a built-in tendency to sit back and let others do the work. The ordained ministries were no longer inherited as they had been in Old Testament times, but they gradually took dominant places in the church's life. Lay people increasingly became spectators. By the Middle Ages, the separation had become so extreme that lay people were hardly considered members of the church at all. People said that those who were ordained had "gone into the church." Sometimes we still hear that kind of language today. Perhaps too often, lay people have been content to let the ordained clergy do the work of ministry on their behalf.

When the Reformation shook the Christian church in the sixteenth century, one of the goals of the reformers was to restore that sense of a shared ministry the first Christians had known. Some of the reformed churches gave up the word *priest* and abolished the position of bishop. Preaching was given a much stronger emphasis, and clergy were sometimes simply called *preachers*. Lay people took a more active role in church life and were chosen to be elders and deacons. But since it was recognized that not everyone had the gift of preaching and that preaching required special training, at least that one ministry within the church continued to take a leadership position. Before long preachers were being called *ministers*, and the ministry of other church members was once again forgotten. Even the "Amen" at the end of prayers became, in many churches, a response made only by the "minister." Instead of being actively involved in worship, congregations usually sat through prayers and sermon alike. The congregation's part was mostly confined to singing hymns, and even for those, people often remained sitting. With such a passive role on Sundays, it is hardly surprising that lay people continued to think of themselves largely as supporters of the ministry of the clergy rather than as ministers in their own right.

The Reformation had a less radical impact on Anglican worship, but Episcopalians have not avoided this way of thinking entirely. They did preserve the ancient ministries of bishops, priests, and deacons. And they did insist that no Eucharist could take place without at least two or three lay people present to play their part, but that part was often reduced to saying a few responses or delegated to a *clerk*. Lay ministry, the priesthood of all believers, was still largely forgotten.

Today all that is changing. A new reformation has been reshaping the Christian churches, and the recovery of lay ministry is a major aspect of that renewal. The Episcopal Church has a unique advantage in this movement because ministry in this church was never confined to one group. Bishops and priests always have had clear and separate ministries, and the role of deacons was never entirely forgotten. The renewal of ministry in the Episcopal Church has recovered the role of deacons and established them widely in a "servant ministry," reaching out to the poor and sick. But the renewal of lay ministry has been the most important aspect of this reformation. Many dioceses have established programs for training lay ministers and parish bulletins often list "all baptized members" as ministers.

The various forms of ministry are most apparent in churches on Sunday morning. An ordained priest may preside over the service, but lay people serve as greeters, ushers, and readers, and often help to distribute communion. Some lay people also serve as choir members or acolytes, while still others may be members of an altar guild, preparing the altar for the service. Others teach the young people or lead adult classes.

But confining ministry to Sunday misses the point. All these Sunday ministries reflect the many ministries carried on by church members during the week. Raising children is a ministry, and so is serving as a nurse, doctor, lawyer or government worker. Whatever role Christians fill in their life during the week can be a ministry, serving others and witnessing in deeds as well as words to the new life given us in baptism. Participating actively in Sunday worship ought to form ways of thinking and acting that shape our whole week. It brings our life into focus, with God at the center, and with no clear line between ministry and worship.

Lay ministry matters in so many significant ways, but it should not be forgotten that, as in so many lines of work, a large percentage of it is just "showing up." Being there when the church gathers for worship is important in and of itself. The church can hardly function as a body if some of its members are missing. Nothing is more discouraging to Christians than finding the church half empty. Simply filling a place in the pews makes a difference. Lay ministry begins with something that simple. Those in attendance on Sunday are strengthened by being there and fortified to go out and be ministers for the rest of the week.

## ORDAINED MINISTRY
### BISHOPS

The New Testament not only speaks of a priesthood of all believers, but also shows us the beginnings of separate ministerial roles that lead to the ordained ministry as we know it today. Jesus, first of all, called twelve to be with him, and they had a special role to play from the very beginning. Jesus sent them out on missions two by two, and gave them authority to heal and to preach. They came to be known as *apostles:* people who are sent out on a mission. Later a larger group of seventy was also sent out, but the twelve continued to provide a leadership role after Jesus' resurrection and during the early days of the church. There is no clear documentation of what happened after that, but by the beginning of the second century it seems to have been taken for granted that leaders in the church were those appointed by the apostles and their successors. The members of this new generation of leaders were called bishops. The Greek word, found in the last books of the Bible, is *episcopos,* which means *overseer.* The name of the Episcopal Church comes from that word and makes it clear that we carry on this same ministry, looking to our bishops, as the successors of the apostles, for a ministry of oversight and leadership.

Down through the centuries, this leadership has been passed from bishop to bishop by a solemn laying on of hands. Sometimes bishops have been chosen by gatherings of clergy, sometimes by the whole membership of the church, and sometimes by kings or popes. But always their authority has come from the laying on of hands by other bishops, going all the way back to the days of the apostles and probably to the apostles themselves. The bishop has become a symbol of the apostolic origins of the church and of our unity with other Christians across time and space.

Perhaps once a year, the bishop visits each parish within his or her diocese to exercise the ministry of chief pastor and representative of the larger church, as the one who unites parishes in a diocese, and dioceses in a worldwide communion. The bishop always presides and preaches during these parish visits. There are bishops in other churches who are seen primarily as administrators, but the Prayer Book makes it clear that in the Episcopal Church a bishop's ministry is to be a "chief priest and pastor" who works to unite the church, to proclaim God's word, and to "guard the faith, unity, and discipline of the whole Church."

An important part of that role, ever since the earliest times, has been the laying on of hands. Just as bishops receive their authority from other bishops through the laying on of hands, so also the other clergy, priests and deacons, are set apart for their ministry by the laying on of hands. At confirmation, the bishop lays hands on the laity as well to confer the gifts they need for lay ministry. Through the bishop, every confirmed member of the church is symbolically united with the "communion of saints," the whole church and all its members in every age.

PRIESTS

The bishop is the chief pastor, but priests are the pastors of each local church. The word *priest* comes from the Greek word *presbyter* (or *elder*) and can also be found in the later books of the New Testament. It seems that the church simply took over the organizational system of the Jewish synagogue, which was governed by a board of elders. The Christian elders, however, were responsible not only for administering the local congregation, but also for presiding at the Lord's Supper in the absence of a bishop. In this role, they represented the whole congregation in its priestly ministry, taking part in Christ's sacrificial offering of himself. So the new Christian priesthood carried on in a new way the priestly ministry of the Old Testament. Now the priest's role was not to offer new sacrifices but to represent, in the Prayer Book's words, the "one, perfect, and sufficient sacrifice" made for us by Christ on the cross on Calvary. So the Episcopal priest, standing at the altar, represents Christ's priesthood to the congregation and the priesthood of the congregation to God. The 1979 Prayer Book speaks of the priest as "the Celebrant," but it is actually the whole congregation that celebrates, and the priest is simply the one who presides at that celebration.

## Deacons

Deacons comprise the third order of ordained ministry. Very early in the life of the church, it became obvious to the apostles that they could not continue to preach the word and still have time to take care of administrative problems. There were church members whose needs were being neglected, and the apostles wisely decided to delegate some of their responsibilities to others. We read in the Book of Acts that they selected seven assistants. Whether we should think of these seven as the first deacons is not clear, but it is certain that deacons were a part of the church almost from the beginning, functioning in a "servant ministry." Today, deacons are often involved in the social ministries of the church, reaching out to the poor and needy in the community, and bringing the needs of the larger community to the attention of the church. Appropriately, deacons often lead the "Prayers of the People," and assist the priest in the celebration of the Eucharist. Deacons assist in preparing the altar and in administering communion. Not every parish has a deacon, but the church is encouraging more members to serve in this ministry, and training programs exist in most dioceses to help people prepare for this role.

In most churches, on most Sundays, leadership of worship remains the role of the priest, who is specially trained and then ordained by the bishop to this ministry of word and sacrament. Lay people usually assist in the different ways we have described, and deacons may assist as well. If you look at the Catechism on pages 855–856 of the Prayer Book, you will see how remarkably similar the definitions of lay ministry are to those of bishops, priests, and deacons. Ministry is shared, and all church members have a ministry to carry out day by day.

## QUESTIONS FOR FURTHER THOUGHT AND DISCUSSION

1. Is it difficult or easy for you to think of yourself as a "minister"? Why?

2. The author describes the apostolic origins of the Episcopal Church. How important are they to you? Do you think such origins are relevant in today's world? If so, how?

3. Refer to pp. 855–856 of the Prayer Book and compare the definitions of lay ministry with those of bishops, priests, and deacons. In what ways are they different? In what ways are they the same?

# How: A Way of Worship

## INCARNATION AND SACRAMENTS

A magazine cartoon some years ago showed a congregation gathered in a church. From high in one corner of the church a band of angels appeared blowing trumpets, indicating, it would seem, the end of the world. Sitting in the pews below, one woman turned to another and said, "My goodness, Mabel, you Episcopalians certainly do like ceremonial!"

Perhaps when the last trumpet does finally blow, there will be Episcopalians who think it is just one more Sunday. Some aspects of the heavenly worship described in the Book of Revelation will certainly be more familiar to Episcopalians than to lots of other Christians. Not many Episcopalians frequently see the clouds of incense and the golden altars, or the harps and trumpets described in the last book of the Bible, but almost all Episcopalians are accustomed to worship that involves sight and sound, candles and vestments, organs and choirs, flowers and crosses, stained glass and even smells (though more often of lilies than incense). These beautiful things are used in an orderly way to praise God.

Here we come to a source of continuing disagreement

among Christians. There are those who feel instinctively that worship should be plain and simple, that it is "showing off" and distracting to embellish worship as Episcopalians tend to do. For many Protestant churches it has been almost an article of faith to declare that such things are wrong, that they are "too Catholic," at odds with the "simple message of the Gospel." And yet, most churches today employ much more ceremony than most churches did in their parents' and grandparents' time. We live in a visual age, and a church that fails to make some appeal to our eyes as well as our ears will fail to hold our attention. We are so accustomed to colorful visual stimulation that even churches with deep-rooted historic objections to ceremony are changing fast. The prejudice against ceremony seems to be fading.

And disliking ceremony is a prejudice, usually based more on an emotional reaction than a reasoned decision. It probably derives from the Reformation effort to restore balance between word and sacrament. The medieval church had become fixated on ceremony: all too often it took the place of faith. Carrying out certain ceremonies was all that mattered. The time came to renew the church and value faith again above forms. The result, in all the reformed churches, was a great and appropriate simplification of Christian worship, brought about only after long and violent battles that left the members of those churches with an emotional distrust of ceremonial. But the reform, as it often does, went too far. Simplification became mere destruction as statues were thrown down, altars demolished, and stained glass windows smashed. In many Protestant churches, all symbols—even crosses—were abandoned. New England meeting houses were deliberately built with no center aisle so that there would be no intersection with the aisle across the front of the church to form a cross on the floor. But times have changed. What the past rejected is now once again appreciated as art, if not always as worship. The descendants of those who smashed the statues centuries ago now stand in line to see the Pieta and buy CDs of medieval chanting. Art does have a part to play in human life.

Even Anglicans sometimes forgot this underlying principle: human beings are both physical and spiritual. We cannot separate the material side of our lives from the spiritual. Most of us recognize the hypocrisy involved when someone who piously goes to church on Sunday then goes to work on Monday in an office in which customers are defrauded and employees are mistreated. Our faith must find physical expression in our everyday lives. If we express our faith on Sunday in material ways and use material things as an expression of our faith, perhaps we will be able to connect our faith with the rest of our lives more easily.

Two words sum up this point of view: one is *incarnation* and the other, *sacrament.* Both are central to an understanding of the way Episcopalians worship. Christian faith begins with the incarnation, the Son of God coming into the world in human flesh and blood. "The Word became flesh," says St. John's Gospel, "and lived among us"(1:14). God did not send us merely good ideas or spiritual notions; God became flesh, outwardly visible to us so that the gospel proclaims not only "what we have heard, what we have seen with our eyes," but also "what we have . . . touched with our hands" (1 John 1:1) Only when God came to us in human flesh could flesh-and-blood human beings fully understand who God is. For Anglicans, the incarnation has always been central. It is no coincidence that Christmas, the celebration of the incarnation, brings with it so many English customs. In Puritan New England, celebrating Christmas was illegal, but Anglicans continued to deck the hall with boughs of holly, stir up the plum pudding, and remember the poor in doing so. In Charles Dickens' famous story, "A Christmas Carol," when Scrooge finally catches the spirit of Christmas, he sends a plump goose to his poorly paid clerk. Faith in an incarnate Savior needs to be expressed in outward and visible ways.

A faith centered on the incarnation is expressed quite naturally through sacraments. The Prayer Book defines sacraments as "outward and visible signs of inward and spiritual grace" (p. 857). Just as God's word is expressed most fully in Jesus, the Son of God made human, so God speaks to us also through other material means. New members are received into the church through baptism, in which water is the outward sign of God's grace at work to renew our lives. Week by week we come to the altar to receive the bread and wine through which the life of Christ comes into our lives. The body of Christ is joined with our bodies, and his life-giving blood courses through our veins and arteries. God's love becomes tangible: we can taste it on our tongues. Being human, we need such evidence. Just as a man and a woman who have fallen in love need to touch each other and hold each other, need to feel physically the invisible love they know, so human beings need outward expressions of their faith. Jesus himself gave the disciples bread and wine as evidence of his presence with them. He also laid his hands on the sick and anointed blind eyes with spittle. The incarnate Savior inevitably used sacramental means to make God's love and healing clear.

So it was natural, from the earliest days of the church, for Christians to use sacramental expressions of their faith in their worship. When Roman officials in the second century came to arrest the members of a Christian congregation they made an inventory of the church's possessions, which included candles, plates, cups, vestments, and books. Even under persecution, Christians felt a need to accumulate these materials to enrich their worship. When persecution ended, Christians indulged that impulse openly by building great churches and embellishing them with mosaic tile and elaborate vestments. Yes, there can be too much of such things—and eventually there was. We can spend so much energy on the outward expression of our faith that we lose all sight of the inward. But rather than go from one extreme to the other, it seems best to balance both aspects of our existence. There is nothing to be gained by denying the reality of the physical world and the bodies that God created and called good. A church that shuns material things denies this basic truth: that the God who created material things used those same things to become known to us. It is fitting and inevitable that such a God be worshiped with and through outward and visible forms.

## POSTURE AND GESTURE

Let's get down to cases. A sacramental faith is one that makes an appropriate use of ceremonial. In an Episcopal church, ceremonies are not there simply to impress us, much less to confuse us, but to involve us and speak to us. No doubt they can be overdone, but there are three very simple guidelines by which to judge them: ceremonies are good if they involve Christians in common action, if they help make clear what we are doing and why, and if they have been used widely by Christians from the earliest days.

Think, for example, of the various ways people participate in the Sunday service as readers, ushers, and choristers, or as acolytes who carry a cross or torch and assist at the altar. Certainly we could hold a service in which one worship leader did it all, but how would that involve us? From the earliest days, Christians have understood worship as a communal activity in which all have a part to play. We are not an audience, but a team, working together in and out of church. Such a vision of the church is complicated and may involve some training and rehearsals to be done well. There are always some who would rather not be involved, but Christianity as we understand it is an active faith and does ask us to get involved and express our faith in outward and active ways.

At the very simplest level, this involvement is expressed by the changes of posture that so many newcomers to the Episcopal Church find surprising. Sitting, standing, and kneeling express participation. They mark the difference between the audience in a movie theater and the congregation in a church. A generation ago, Episcopalians were taught to kneel to pray, stand to praise, and sit to listen, but customs are changing. Medieval Christians knelt through most of the service because penitence was so strongly emphasized, and the service was conducted in Latin which few understood. But the first Christians spent much more time on their feet because praise was their primary focus. So today, as we attempt to find a better balance between penitence and praise, we are moving back toward the behavior patterns of the early church, kneeling less and standing more.

But kneeling remains important. So Episcopal churches usually have "kneelers" that fold down from the pew in front or hassocks of some sort on which church members can kneel. Most Episcopalians, when they first come into church for a service, fold down the kneeler or pull out a hassock and kneel for a few minutes of prayer. Kneeling is a posture of humility and is always appropriate for prayer. The Prayer Book suggests that we kneel for the General Confession when we ask forgiveness for our sins. Episcopalians are divided at present about kneeling for the intercession, consecration, and communion. Some think that it is most appropriate to express humility and penitence. Others believe that we honor God best by standing, as we would if someone important came into the room. One view reflects the medieval custom, and the other that of the early church. It is not unusual to see some members of the congregation standing while others kneel. Unity is important, but it is also important for worshipers to adopt the posture that feels most natural for them. There's room for differences in some things, so long as what we do is not disruptive. Those who choose to stand while others are kneeling may move to the side or toward the back so as not to block others' sight lines. Standing for prayer is a better alternative to kneeling than sitting in a hunched over posture.

Sitting is always an appropriate posture for listening; the Prayer Book directs the congregation to sit during the Old Testament and Epistle readings and during the sermon. If announcements are being made, of course, the congregation sits to listen to them and, sometimes, to the choir singing an anthem. The only exception to the sit-to-listen rule comes when it's time to hear the Gospel read. Christians have always stood to hear it read as a way of expressing the honor due to Our Lord. After all, the Gospel is the record of Jesus' own words and actions. In churches where the Gospel book is carried down into the center of the congregation to be read, all members of the congregation should turn toward the book.

Standing is the posture that expresses honor and praise. We tend almost instinctively to stand when someone important comes into a room. In the same way, we stand when the gospel is read and when a procession of clergy and others come into the church to begin the service. We also would stand to pledge allegiance to the flag, and the recital of the Creed is the Christian equivalent of that. It is equally natural to stand for hymns, because most of them are expressions of faith and praise. Standing to pray is also perfectly appropriate. The early Christians made a point of the difference between standing for prayer as they did, and kneeling as many pagans did. "We stand," they said, "because we have been set free as children of God and so we do not grovel like slaves."

But freedom also must allow for variety. The point should be made again that a congregation is made up of individuals who come from many backgrounds and are accustomed to expressing themselves in different ways. If standing for prayer seems unnatural, or if kneeling for prayer is uncomfortable, nothing is gained if we feel forced to conform. It is also true that those who are unable to stand or kneel should always feel free to sit if necessary.

Closely connected to posture is the use of gesture. Some Episcopalians, for example, bow their heads when a processional cross is carried by or when they hear the name of Jesus in a prayer or in a hymn. Church members also commonly bow to the cross before entering their pews or when passing in front of the altar. Others genuflect (kneel briefly on one knee) at such times. Such behavior is very biblical: St. Paul wrote that "at the name of Jesus every knee should bend" (Philippians 2:10) and the Book of Revelation speaks of how the elders in heaven "fall before the one who is seated on the throne" in worship (Revelation 4:10). Making the sign of the cross is another gesture commonly used by some. To trace the cross on yourself by moving your hand from your head to your heart, and then from your left shoulder to the right one, is a way of making a physical response to the end of the Creed (sealing the Creed to ourselves with the cross), and to the absolution and the blessing. It's a way of taking that benediction to ourselves, saying "Amen" to it in an outward way.

Praying or singing with an upraised hand or hands is another gesture often seen in Episcopal services. Although such gestures are new to the Episcopal Church and are associated with the renewal movement and its more emotional styles of prayer and church music, the holding up of hands in prayer can be seen in ancient frescos depicting Christians at worship. In fact, in one of his letters St. Paul speaks of "lifting up holy hands" in prayer (1 Timothy 2:8). The gesture is very similar to that used by many priests as they preside at the Eucharist and seems to be a natural way for lay people to express their own priesthood.

All these personal gestures are only useful if they feel natural to each individual. Some of us are naturally less demonstrative than others and feel uncomfortable with the hugs and kisses that others take for granted. No one should feel compelled to use gestures that seem unnatural or uncomfortable, but many find the use of some gestures helpful in worship. Some of us express ourselves better by actions than by words. We are all different, and those differences deserve respect; complete uniformity in our worship would ignore our God-given individuality.

The clergy are different too; some give blessings with large and obvious gestures, while others may make smaller signs or simply raise one hand. Some clergy are more formal in their movements and others less formal. The Episcopal Church has no official standards in these areas, trusting the clergy to adopt patterns that are appropriate and helpful in creating an atmosphere of reverence in the presence of God.

Before moving on, it may be worth recalling the story Jesus told of two men who went up to the temple to pray. Both men remained standing, but one told God of his achievements while the other "standing far off, would not even look up to heaven, but was beating his breast and saying, 'God, be merciful to me, a sinner!'" (St. Luke 18:9). He expressed penitence not by kneeling, but by the place where he stood, his downcast eyes, and the motion of his arm. Posture and gesture are important means of expression, but what we do, and how we do it, are conditioned largely by our culture, upbringing, and local customs. Our postures and gestures merge into a very slow and stately dance; we use our bodies to express our thoughts and feelings more fully than words can. As a matter of fact, liturgical dance is seen much more often in churches in recent years. Just as choirs offer more intricate music than most of us can produce, so also liturgical dance troops offer the beauty of rhythmical body movements beyond what most of us are capable of. Yet all members of the congregation are invited to join in the music and movement of the liturgy to the degree that they are able. We all have a part to play according to our interests and ability. There is no one "right" way or "wrong" way—with the exception of allowing ourselves to become mere spectators.

## VESTURE

What we wear and why we wear it are also conditioned by culture and custom. Pictures of baseball crowds in the 1920s and 1930s show men sitting in the stands wearing jackets and ties, with their Stetsons and fedoras on their heads. Not many dress that way today for a ball game. Nor do people dress as formally for church services as they did a generation ago, when men generally wore ties and women always wore hats. And just as the congregation's dress has changed, so has the clergy's, though less radically. That difference between the changing patterns of dress in the congregation and among the clergy helps explain where vestments came from in the first place. So far as we can tell, the clergy and people dressed alike in the early days of the church. Jewish priests wore elaborate vestments in the temple, but the early Christians, with no tradition to guide them, seem to have dressed like everyone else. As time went on, however, styles changed and most Christians changed with the fashions—except the clergy. Somehow it seemed wrong for the clergy to be too "trendy," so they continued to dress in the "old fashioned" style of their predecessors. Eventually the clerical style of dress became so completely out of date that their special vestments became associated only with the church. But these unique vestments were simply the normal street dress of the late Roman Empire.

In the sixteenth century, many reformers tried to simplify clerical garb and rejected the traditional vestments in favor of the street dress or academic robes of their own time. Half a millennium later, these, too, have become "traditional," but the black "pulpit gowns" of Protestant churches, like the black cassock and white surplice often seen in the Episcopal Church, are simply the ordinary dress of another era.

Vesture has seen striking changes in recent years. Not long ago, the vestments used in the Episcopal Church were controversial. Traditional vestments were widely used, but many objected to them as "too Roman." That division of opinion seems to have faded now; traditional vestments are used widely, but in the process they have seen a number of changes. They are often more colorful, employing a wider variety of materials and patterns, but are sometimes also simpler than those of an earlier age.

What was the street dress of the Roman Empire? "Toga parties" have made us familiar with one variation on the theme: a loose sheet of cloth thrown over the shoulder or wrapped loosely around the body. We have all seen statues of Greek and Roman gods and goddesses, as well as statesmen and other citizens of the classical world, robed in this way. A somewhat more formally dressed Roman citizen would probably have worn a long white robe called an *alb*. On cooler days he would add a poncho-like, heavier piece of material called a *chasuble* (the Latin word meant " little house"). Episcopal clergy today often begin vesting by putting on a long, white alb, and belting it with a cord called a *cincture*. Next they drape a long band of cloth around the neck and tuck it under the cincture; this is the scarf the Romans called a *stola*, which is now called a stole. Over all these goes a chasuble, a garment almost circular in shape, with a hole in the center for the head. The stole and chasuble make generous use of color, depending on the season of the liturgical year. Over the centuries, the church developed explanations for these vestments that had nothing to do with their real origins but rather gave them "mystical meanings." The chasuble, for example, was said to express the virtue of love or charity that covers everything else. The stole symbolized a yoke joining the wearer to Christ in a shared ministry. Such "meanings" were made up long after the fact, but there is nothing wrong with thinking about vestments that way. St. Paul, after all, urges us to "put on Christ," and the meanings associated with the traditional vestments may help us remember that calling.

While the traditional vestments are probably most common today, many Episcopal clergy still prefer the sixteenth-century version, the long black cassock covered with a white surplice. For the Eucharist, the colored stole is worn over the surplice and for other services a black *tippet* (like a stole but usually wider) is worn, sometimes with an academic hood. Most clergy wear the cassock and surplice with the stole or tippet and hood, or the alb and stole, when they are assisting at the Eucharist or conducting other services.

Bishops dress like priests for the Eucharist, but usually wear a double-pointed hat called a *miter*, which is a sort of symbol of the tongues of fire that descended on the apostles' heads at Pentecost. Bishops often (and priests sometimes) also wear a colored vestment called a *cope*, which is thrown over the shoulders like a cape and held together at the front with a clasp.

Bishops may carry a staff shaped like a shepherd's crook as a symbol of their role as chief pastor. Deacons most often wear either an alb or a cassock and surplice, with a stole over one shoulder and knotted under the opposite arm.

Lay people who assist at the service as choir members and acolytes usually wear vestments based on those of the clergy or of medieval monks. The alb or the cassock and surplice are probably most common, but choir members especially these days often wear robes based on academic or monastic garb rather than clerical vestments. As vestments become more common in the non-liturgical churches, designs have begun to reflect a wide range of influences: the Japanese kimono, African tribal costumes, or even, it would sometimes seem, the sorcerer's apprentice. Simplicity is still valued, but the desire to emphasize the joy of worship leads to a much wider variety of color and style. It should be noted that the Episcopal Church has no set requirements in this area. The Prayer Book refers only to stoles, and even then says nothing about shape or color. Churches and clergy are given great freedom to respond to ethnic traditions and other special circumstances and do what seems appropriate in their particular situations.

One final note: vestments are not intended to draw attention to the individuals wearing them or to emphasize personal idiosyncrasies. Church vestments are intended to conceal individual differences and identify clergy by office, not to tell us "this is Jim Smith" but that "this is a priest." Vestments should have a certain simplicity and dignity because they are an offering to God's glory, not to that of individuals. Embroiderers and other artists can use their God-given gifts to make vestments for God's service, just as musicians offer music and artisans design stained glass windows. Christian worship can use all gifts to praise and honor the One who gives them to us.

## OTHER CEREMONIAL ASPECTS OF WORSHIP

Ceremonial is a subject that includes much more than movements and vestments. Crosses and candles are in wide use, though once they, too, were controversial. Candles were necessities in the early days of the church since light bulbs had not been invented. Even the Puritans used candles in church, though they placed them only on the pulpit and in sconces on the walls. Like everything else, however, what once was simply practical became traditional, and Christians debated how many candles they should have on the altar: two, six, eight, or some other number. In most Episcopal churches today there are two candles on the altar. Often there are six more on a shelf behind the altar, or two seven-branch candlesticks. Sometimes standing candles are placed beside the altar and often six are placed around a coffin at a funeral service. At Christmas and Easter, churches light even more candles to add to the festive atmosphere. For many Episcopalians, lighting and extinguishing the candles is a mystical symbol of the beginning and end of the service. Some church members to this day will not move at the end of the service until the candles are extinguished. While others may laughingly refer to them as "fire worshipers," they gain a quiet time for personal prayers before leaving the church.

Why is it that candles seem so much more appropriate to formal occasions than electric bulbs? Whatever it is, we all enjoy candles on the table in our homes at special times and on the cake at a birthday party. The flame seems to suggest life, and its movement adds mystery. For Christians, the candle represents Christ as the light of the world. Many churches place an especially large candle near the font during the Easter season, having lighted it at a vigil service on Easter Eve. This *paschal* candle, representing the light of the risen Christ, is then lit again at baptisms. Small replicas of it may be given to those who are baptized or to the parents or godparents of baptized infants.

Flowers bring a beautiful part of God's creation inside the church. Lilies at Easter and poinsettias at Christmas are traditional but certainly not required. Most churches don't put flowers in the church during Lent. Flowers are also brought to the church for weddings and funerals, sometimes so abundantly that they get in the way of the service. Churches often establish local guidelines to prevent difficulties, and those making plans for such services should always ask what the customs are.

More exotic, but less so than a generation ago, is the use of incense. Styles change, and what once seemed dangerously "Roman" now may seem dangerously "New Age." But incense has an ancient heritage and is one of the most biblical additions to worship. In the Old Testament there are dozens of references to the use of incense, and several in the New Testament. The prophet Malachi, for example, quotes God as commending the Gentiles for honoring God with incense (1:11) while the New Testament tells us that the Magi brought incense as a gift for the infant Jesus (Matthew 2:11) and that the prayers of the saints in heaven rise like incense (Revelation 5:8, 8:3). Smells have a deep emotional resonance for most people, conjuring up memories of autumn leaves, new-mown grass, and Thanksgiving at Grandma's house. Such emotions kick in heavily both for and against the use of incense in church, and make its use too controversial for many churches. Nonetheless, it is an aspect of worship in some parishes.

"Smells and bells" are beloved by some and offensive to others. The bells in question are not those in the steeple, which seem uncontroversial, but those at the altar. They are relics of the days when the church's services were in Latin and the bells were used to tell people what was happening. Absorbed in their own devotions, or distracted by wandering thoughts, they might not have been looking up when the priest held up the consecrated bread and cup for them to see. Since few in those days received communion, they would have missed what they came to see. So an acolyte or assistant would ring a bell to get their attention. With services in English and frequent communion, the practical value of such bell ringing is long gone, but bells, like candles, add a certain enchantment for many. Where they are used, it is to mark the solemn moments of the service, such as the beginning of the prayer of consecration and the words of Jesus at the Last Supper. Sometimes a tower bell peals at such moments, and sometimes the organist plays bell-like tones, but more often a small gong or set of bells placed near the altar is used.

## SILENCE

Silence is not exactly a ceremonial aspect, but it is a vital element in worship. Perhaps silence is what begins when ceremonial comes to an end. The God we worship is known to us in words, sacraments, and ceremonial, but God is far beyond these things. We sometimes hear God best while practicing silence. The prophet Elijah, waiting for God, endured wind, earthquake, and fire, but God was in none of them. When they had passed by, there followed "a sound of sheer silence" in which God spoke (1 Kings 19:12). At a climactic moment in St. John's vision of heaven, "there was silence in heaven for about half an hour" (Revelations 8:1). All too few modern Christians would know what to do with silence for that length of time, though many have found its value through Eastern religions. But the Book of Common Prayer commends it frequently, and more and more churches do try to incorporate it as a regular element in their worship. In a world that assails us constantly with noise, a few moments of silence can be a great gift. Times of silence before and after the service, before and after communion, and after readings from the Bible can provide a welcome opportunity to offer our own prayers, or to reflect on what has been said. But simply to be quiet in God's presence is a communion that no words can express.

The use of outward and visible elements can do much to enrich our worship, but they can also be over-emphasized and distracting. Anglicans have always tried to find a balance between too much and too little, and balance is vitally important. Silence and simplicity remind us, as Solomon knew, that a God who cannot be contained in the heaven of heavens can surely never be contained in houses built by human hands (1 Kings 8:27). It is right to offer the best that we have, and equally important to recognize the limits and total inadequacy of all human efforts to devise patterns of worship worthy of our Creator.

## QUESTIONS FOR FURTHER
## THOUGHT AND DISCUSSION

1. Do you agree with the author's opinion that the "prejudice" against "ceremony" is fading? Are you attracted to the ceremony of the Episcopal Church? Why or why not?

2. The author speaks to the need for a balance between the outward expression of our faith through material means and the development of our inner lives. How well does your church achieve this balance? What suggestions would you make to improve it?

3. Are you comfortable with the various postures of worship—sitting, kneeling, standing? Do you think it is more appropriate to stand or to kneel during the intercession, consecration, and communion? Why?

# The Christian Year

Seasons are a part of almost everyone's experience. Even if we live in parts of the world where snow never falls or ice never melts, parts of the year will be known as rainy or snowy or dry. Just as there are natural sequences of weather, there are sequences in the heavens too. The phases of the moon mark out four-week cycles, while the stars and planets wheel through the night sky in a predictable annual pattern. Every human society has ceremonies to mark these changing seasons. And each human being has his or her own special times: we celebrate our birthdays and anniversaries and mark the coming of age of children. In the ancient world, some societies thought of life as a wheel that turned through seedtime and harvest time, yet forever remained the same. Hebrew society, on the other hand, was formed in the desert experience of nomads for whom the cycle of growth and decay was unimportant. For them, history was marked by unique events such as the escape from Egypt. Though Passover later became connected with spring time and planting celebrations, it remained rooted in historic events. The Jewish people saw life not as a meaningless cycle but as a journey with a beginning and an end, something with purpose and a goal. God was at work in their lives, revealing a purpose through historic events and prophetic speech.

Celebrating a "Christian Year" is a natural result of our Jewish heritage. The first Christians grew up as Jews who celebrated the historical events of the Jewish calendar. Christ's death and resurrection were grounded in the story of the Passover. The coming of the Holy Spirit took place on the Jewish festival called Pentecost. In the sixteenth century, during the turmoil of the Reformation, much of the church's rich tradition was rejected. Customs such as the Yule log, boar's head, and Christmas tree were considered frivolous and pagan—as indeed they were originally. For many years it was against the law to celebrate Christmas in the New England colonies, and people went to jail for doing so. Today, of course, few people, even atheists, are so hard-hearted as to deny their children some kind of festivity. Christmas is promoted by merchants even more eagerly than by missionaries. The card and candy companies have developed a cycle of secular celebrations that moves from Halloween to Thanksgiving, Christmas, the New Year, Valentine's Day, Easter, Mother's Day, and the Fourth of July. The ancient Christian Year, rich in meaning and designed to deepen our faith, is twisted and obscured by the relentless promotion of what have become secular holidays. Nevertheless, the Episcopal Church has set its life in the framework of the Christian Year. Every church service is shaped by that calendar since the prayers and lessons are assigned to it according to the theme of the season. Hymns are not assigned but are chosen with the same themes in mind. Flowers and vestments and many other customs also reflect these seasonal changes.

What is this pattern? In brief, the Episcopal Church calendar includes six major seasons: Advent, Christmas, Epiphany, Lent, Easter, and Pentecost. This sequence of seasons has two focal points. Easter in the spring is one, and Christmas in mid-winter is the other. The date of Easter varies with the moon, but the date of Christmas is always December 25. The problem with this arrangement is that the number of Sundays between Christmas and Easter varies. If there are more Sundays before Easter, there will be fewer afterwards. So the post-Christmas or "Epiphany" season and the Pentecost season can fluctuate by a month or more. The church's solution to this problem is to provide a continuous set of readings for those two seasons that begins after Epiphany, is interrupted by the Lent-Easter season, and picks up again after Pentecost. These Sundays are sometimes called the "Sundays in ordinary time," the Sundays that have no special event to commemorate. On those days we read through the Bible in a continuous pattern. Scattered through these Sundays are a number of saints' days and other special days. Let's look at all of these in turn.

## ADVENT

Just as there is no starting point on a wheel, so there is no single, logical place for the year to begin. All of us are aware of several years with different starting points: a school year beginning in late summer, a financial year that often begins on July 1 or some other date, and a secular year that begins on January 1. If we have Jewish friends, we know that their year begins with Rosh Hashanah in September, and if we live in a major city, we may be aware of a Chinese New Year that comes long after January 1. For Christians, however, the year begins with the season of Advent, the four weeks in which we prepare for Christmas. Since Christmas celebrates Christ's birth, the preparation for that day does form a logical starting point. Beginnings bring endings to mind as well, and as we prepare to celebrate Christ's first coming, it is natural to think also of his promised last coming at the end of time. Advent, as a result, has a variety of themes. To prepare for any celebration involves a good deal of work: cleaning house, preparing food, and buying gifts. This may be hard work, but we enjoy it because of the celebration we anticipate. Advent is also a penitential season, a time to remember our sins and seek forgiveness. But a certain joyfulness inevitably mixes in as we prepare for Christ to come. One familiar Advent hymn, dating from the ninth century, calls on Christ to "disperse the gloomy clouds of night" and ends each verse with the refrain, "Rejoice! Rejoice! Emmanuel shall come to thee, O Israel!"

The most familiar custom of the season is probably the Advent wreath, four candles in a setting of greens. It is a custom any individual or family can use at home very easily, lighting one candle each day through the first week, two candles each day through the second week and so on, with a simple prayer such as the Collect for that Sunday. The Advent Collects are in the Prayer Book on pages 159–160 (traditional language) and 211–212 (contemporary version). Children enjoy opening a window each day on their Advent calendars to reveal a new scene or Bible verse. Some Christians also reenact the nativity by placing the figures of the Christmas creche at a distance from the place where they will be on Christmas. They move Mary and Joseph a little closer each day, bringing them to the proper place on December 24, Christmas Eve. The Christ child and shepherds are added on Christmas Day itself.

Two different traditions are followed in the Episcopal Church concerning the seasonal color of Advent. Some churches adhere to the medieval Roman custom of purple vestments and altar hangings. Purple was a royal color in ancient times, and the use of purple in Advent may be thought of as preparing the throne room for the coming of our king, but it has often been called a penitential color because of its dark and somber tone. Alternatively, many churches follow the ancient English custom of using blue in Advent. Blue symbolizes heaven and is also associated with the Virgin Mary, so Advent may be seen as Mary's season and the season when heaven comes to earth. Candles in the Advent wreath can be either blue or purple—or even white or whatever is available.[1]

## CHRISTMAS

Christmas needs no promotion, but it is often in need of explanation. It is celebrated world wide by people who have no idea at all of its origins. Japan, for example, is a country whose population is about 1 percent Christian and where many citizens have never met a Christian face to face. Nonetheless, Christmas is celebrated everywhere, perhaps because employees usually receive very generous year-end bonuses. Merchants have learned to use Christmas as a way to move the money into their tills. Christian missionaries tell of being asked by civic leaders to explain the meaning of the event to the community—which they are always glad to do.

Even in America, many Americans don't understand Christmas, partly because some Christians come from traditions that have long opposed the celebration, but also because merchants promote it for non-theological reasons. The commercial Christmas celebration begins not only well into Advent but back toward Halloween. Church members who insist on waiting until the day itself to celebrate are looked on as somewhat eccentric. In the Christian Year, however, Christmas begins on December 25, or the eve of that day, and continues to January 6, when the coming of the wise men is

---

1. Another Roman Catholic custom is the use of a pink or rose-colored candle on the third Sunday of Lent. This use of a lighter color symbolizes a lightening of the Advent penitence. Unless people are deep in penitence—unusual in this era—there seems little reason for it.

celebrated. Most Americans sing about the twelve days of Christmas, even if they do it ahead of time and pull down their trees two or three days after Christmas. The twelve days of Christmas, however, should be a wonderful time of celebration if we have not worn ourselves out by celebrating in advance. Some church members, following the Jewish Hanukkah custom, spread out their gift giving over the whole twelve days. Others place a white candle in the center of the Advent wreath and continue to light it until the twelfth night.

Many Christmas traditions have a pagan origin, and that is not surprising. The celebration takes place on December 25 not because that is the actual date of Christ's birth—a date no one knows—but because Christians incorporated traditions from pagan festivals in northern Europe at the time of the winter solstice. Candles are part of the festival because it is the darkest time of the year, when pagan people prayed for the rebirth of the sun. Evergreen trees, holly, and ivy were used for decoration because they were the only remaining signs of life in a bleak winter landscape. Christians adapted these symbols, taking over the pagan festival without upsetting those who, quite naturally, were reluctant to give up their traditional ceremonies.

The color of Christmas, as for most of the festival seasons, is white.

## EPIPHANY

Epiphany sometimes seems to be a kind of Christmas leftover, but it has the potential to be one of the most important seasons. Its themes of mission and conversion are central to the life of the church. We begin Epiphany by remembering the wise men or Magi. Though they are often shown on Christmas cards, they may not have arrived in Bethlehem until long after Jesus' birth. The gospel says they found Mary and Joseph and the Christ child by entering a house, not a stable, and Herod, having asked the wise men when the star appeared, found it necessary to kill all the children in Bethlehem under the age of two. It may be rushing things to remember them a mere twelve days after Christmas!

Nor are the wise men simply a bit of exotic trimming on the Christmas tale; they symbolize the coming of all nations to worship Christ. The shepherds presumably were Jewish; the wise men were not. We have no idea where they came from, but it is appropriate that they are often shown as being of different races. If we divide the world between Jews and Gentiles, as the Jews traditionally did, the wise men, like most modern Christians, were Gentiles. Had they not come, we might not be Christians. They represent us. And their gifts speak of a profound understanding of Christ. The first gift, gold, is a symbol of wealth. Like the offertory in the Eucharist, the gold says that all we have comes from God and is to be offered. Frankincense, the second gift, is a symbol of worship. The smoke of incense rises and has often seemed to worshipers to represent their prayers ascending to God's throne. This child, unlike all others, is to be worshiped. And the third gift, myrrh, was an ointment used to anoint bodies for burial. When Jesus was taken down from the cross, Joseph of Arimathea brought myrrh and spices to anoint Jesus' body before it was sealed in the tomb. This king was born to die.

Important as these symbolic gifts and this visit may be, the Eastern Church has always focused the Epiphany season not on the wise men, but on Jesus' baptism, celebrated the following Sunday. The increased emphasis on baptism in the 1979 Prayer Book brings this day into greater prominence. The wise men came from distant lands, and Jesus' great commission to his disciples was to go to all nations and baptize (Matthew 28:19). Epiphany, then, is the season of mission, and baptism is central to its meaning. The remaining weeks of the season give us a capsule view of Jesus' ministry with stories of his teaching, healing, and miracles. The word *epiphany* means "manifestation" or "showing." Through this season Christ's ministry and mission and glory is shown forth or made manifest. It is a good time for teaching about mission and for working on projects related to mission and evangelism.

The last Sunday after the Epiphany always brings us the story of Christ's *transfiguration*. On a mountaintop, Peter, James, and John, the three leaders among the apostles, saw Jesus in radiant glory. That brief glimpse of glory and shining light summarizes the Epiphany season and prepares us for the following season of Lent. A nice custom on this last Sunday in Epiphany is to use the word *Alleluia* as much as possible. It is not used in Lent, so this provides an opportunity to "get it out of our system." In the Eastern Orthodox Church it has been customary to paint the word *Alleluia* on a board and bury it, digging it up again at Easter. It is a graphic way of making the point. Episcopal churches usually content themselves with singing hymns like "Alleluia! Sing to Jesus" and "Ye Watchers and Ye Holy Ones" with their repeated *Alleluias*.

The day of Epiphany and the Sunday following are white festivals. The remainder of the season introduces us to the color green, the color of life and growing things. It is the usual color of the church as it is the usual color of the world around us.

## LENT

In the early centuries of the church's life, preparing for baptism was a primary activity. To be baptized was a radical commitment. Persecution could break out at any time, and Christians lived with the threat of torture and death. None were baptized who did not fully understand the commitment they were making. Often, they would spend three years preparing for it—the amount of time we normally expect now of people preparing to be ordained. Baptisms normally took place at Easter so that the candidates could be joined with Christ in his death and share at the same time in his resurrection. So the last weeks before Easter became a time of intensive preparation for baptism through prayer, fasting, and study. Most important of all was the renunciation of sin. The new Christian was renouncing the old way of life in order to be born to a new way.

The period before Easter has gradually taken on the same character for all Christians. It has become a time for renewed commitment and self-discipline. As a part of that self-discipline, Christians abstain from certain foods and luxuries to help them remember how much Christ gave up for us. They also devote themselves more fully to prayer and charity. It seems odd that in an affluent society we downplay the renunciation of luxuries and emphasize instead the need to pray, study the Bible, and serve others. These are good practices, but we will find it hard to take on more until we have given up other things. One fewer movie a week or one fewer meal at the local fast food restaurant would not only improve our physical health, but our spiritual health as well. We could then give time and money more generously to others, and to our own prayer and spiritual growth.

Often a heaviness and gloom seems to hang over Lent, but it should not be like that. The word *Lent* itself comes from the Anglo-Saxon word for spring, the time when the days *lengthen*. As we approach the spring equinox and Easter day, our lives should be filled with light as we come closer to Christ's light. Although many churches still use purple vestments and hangings for Lent with their dark colors, other Episcopal churches follow the ancient English custom of using unbleached linen or monks cloth. This light, simple material gives a church a spring feeling, exactly what Lent is for: a spiritual spring cleaning that reorders and renews our lives. During Lent the crosses and holy pictures are covered, in Roman tradition with purple material, and in the English (or "Sarum"[2] tradition, with monks cloth. In the Sarum custom a simple wooden cross, painted red, replaces the brass or silver cross on the altar as well as the processional cross.

Some of the Sundays in Lent have taken on a special character because of the readings assigned to them. The second Sunday in Lent, for example, is "Abraham Sunday" because the Old Testament reading that day always speaks of Abraham. Some churches make a point of serving milk and honey at the coffee hour on that Sunday since Abraham was called to go to Canaan, a land flowing with milk and honey.

In the same way, the fourth Sunday in Lent is sometimes celebrated as "Mothering Sunday." The readings used on that Sunday until the 1979 Prayer Book always spoke of "Jerusalem . . . the mother of us all." In medieval England, apprentices were given time off on that Sunday to go home to visit their mothers. They would bring bunches of spring flowers and their mothers would make a special fruit cake called *simnel* cake. A number of Episcopal churches still mark the occasion with flowers for mothers and simnel cake at the coffee hour for everyone. Such small traditions can help fix themes from the lessons in our minds and add a pleasant element to our life together.

## HOLY WEEK

From the earliest times, the week before Easter has been a period of very special services. The Gospels give us detailed

---

2. The predominant English customs before the Reformation were those of Salisbury Cathedral, known as "Sarum."

information on the last week of Jesus' ministry, and it was very natural for the church to attempt to live through that week year by year with services commemorating those events. When Constantine ended the persecution of the Christian church early in the fourth century, he made it possible for Christians to travel freely. Those who went on pilgrimages to the Holy Land reported back that they found Christians in Jerusalem still holding services in Holy Week based on the events of that week in Jesus' life. On Palm Sunday, for example, they gathered on the Mount of Olives and went in procession into the city carrying palms.

This is not the place to trace the development of these services through the ages, but it may be helpful to describe briefly the services of this week in the Book of Common Prayer. These days are important: four of the eight days from Palm Sunday to Easter have special liturgies. Ash Wednesday is the only other day in Lent with a special liturgy.

On Palm Sunday, the first day of this week, the Prayer Book furnishes a blessing for the palms and prayers for a procession. In many churches, this procession begins outside the church in a courtyard or parish hall where palms are blessed. The whole congregation then processes into the church carrying palms, just as the crowd on the first Palm Sunday processed into Jerusalem. In some communities otherwise separated churches gather together in some central place for the blessing of palms and then process to their different churches for the remainder of the service. The Gospel account of Jesus' arrest, trial, and death is read on Palm Sunday. The story is a long one, but it comes alive when readers speak the roles, leaving the congregation to take the part of the crowd, crying out "Crucify him!"

On Wednesday of Holy Week, or at the end of the Maundy Thursday service, some churches hold a service called Tenebrae. This simple service of readings and prayers ends when the church lights are extinguished. The contrast between darkness and light is a recurring theme of Holy Week.

Maundy Thursday is the name given to the fifth day of the week in the English tradition—or Holy Thursday in the Roman tradition. The word *maundy* comes from the Latin word *mandare,* or "commandment" because this is the day that Jesus, at the Last Supper, gave his disciples "a new commandment, that you love one another" (John 13:34). Jesus demonstrated the spirit of this commandment by washing his disciples' feet, so there may be a ceremonial foot washing at this service. Jesus humbled himself to serve others, as we also should learn to do. At the end of the service the altar is often stripped and left bare so that the church on Good Friday is barren of all ornamentation.

Good Friday, the day on which Jesus was crucified, is one of two days (the other is Saturday of Holy Week) when communion is not celebrated. The services of the day are simple and plain, consisting of prayers, readings, and meditations with hymns. Communion may be distributed from the bread and wine consecrated the day before, but many churches omit even this. It is a day when we are strongly reminded that we cannot save ourselves. All we can do has been done for us by God in Christ acting on our behalf. It is a day for prayer, and thoughtfulness, and silence.

By contrast with Good Friday, Holy Saturday (or Easter Even) is the day that gives us the most elaborate and beautiful service of the whole year. In the early church it began after sundown and continued through the night. The service began with the lighting of a new fire with flint and steel. The new fire, representing the light of the risen Christ, was kindled outside the church and then carried in and used to light a special paschal candle that would continue to burn through the whole Easter season. After the lighting of the candle, a long series of readings began, tracing the plan of God from the Garden of Eden down through the prophecies of the Old Testament. Those who had been prepared during Lent were baptized and often confirmed. The service ended with the celebration of the Eucharist at which the newly baptized would receive communion for the first time.

Modern Christians are seldom challenged to keep the Easter Vigil through the whole night. Instead, the Easter Vigil may be held at sundown on Saturday or in the middle of the night or even at dawn of Easter Day. As in the early days of the church, a new fire is kindled and carried into a darkened church, then the paschal candle is lighted, and a series of readings leads up to baptisms or the renewal of baptismal vows by the whole congregation. The first Eucharist of Easter may follow immediately or, if the Vigil service has been held on Saturday evening, it may end without the Eucharist so that all may come together to celebrate that on Easter morning.

## EASTER

The center of the church's year is Easter Day.[3] It is the resurrection of Jesus Christ from the dead that lies at the center of Christian faith. The resurrection, St. Paul wrote to the church in Corinth, is of "first importance" (15:3) because "if Christ has not been raised, then our proclamation has been in vain and your faith has been in vain" (15:14). Christ conquered death, enabling Christians to receive the gift of new life through their baptism into Christ's body. In the earliest days of the church, the first day of every week was a time to give

---

3. It should be noticed that the correct title is "Easter Day," not "Easter Sunday." This is the central day of all the days of the year, and not simply a special Sunday. Besides, "Easter Sunday" is redundant; Easter is always a Sunday.

thanks again for this gift since Jesus rose from death on a Sunday. Every Sunday therefore was a celebration of Easter. But no other day in the church year is quite like Easter with its array of flowers, special music, and full churches. It is the greatest day of the church year and the first day in what Christians call the "Queen of Seasons." As the time before Easter became a season of preparation for baptism, so the season after Easter also became an important time, since it was in the forty days after Easter that the risen Lord walked with his disciples and prepared them for their mission to the world. The newly baptized received additional instruction in this post-Easter season of fifty days, ending with the celebration of Pentecost, the day the Holy Spirit filled the disciples with the courage to begin their mission to the world.

The fortieth day after Easter, always a Thursday, is called Ascension Day since the gospel tells us that Jesus was carried up into heaven on that day. Instead of feeling sorrow over the separation, the disciples returned to Jerusalem with "great joy" (Luke 24:52) because Jesus had promised to be with them always. This apparent separation was actually a transformed relationship: Jesus would be present to the whole church throughout the world, rather than confined to the small limits of Palestine. Now Jesus is recognized as Christ or King, ruler of all and our mediator before God's throne. Ascension Day and the ten days afterwards are thought of as a separate season, the shortest one of the Christian Year.

The timing of all these seasons depends, of course, on the date of Easter, and Easter's date is established in the same way as the Jewish Passover. It is, in theory at least, the first Sunday after the first full moon after the first day of spring, or the vernal equinox. But that would be too simple! The date is actually arrived at by an ancient church formula that does not correlate exactly with the spring full moon. Fortunately, most western

Christians agree on how to calculate the date for Easter, but the Orthodox Churches of Russia and Greece and other Eastern countries use a different formula. They often observe Easter on a date several weeks away from the western date. The Book of Common Prayer has tables that provide the western date of Easter for more than a hundred years. If that isn't enough, the 1928 Prayer Book lists Easter dates for the next six thousand years! We might hope that long before that, Christians will have been able to agree on a common date and maybe even find one that is fixed on the same Sunday, perhaps the first or second Sunday in April.

The name *Easter*, like *Lent*, comes from an Anglo-Saxon word. It probably derives from the name of an Anglo-Saxon goddess Oestre, whose feast day came in the spring. The church's best vestments, white or gold, are used for Easter Day, and white remains in use throughout the season.

## PENTECOST

Fifty days after Jesus' resurrection, the disciples assembled in what may have been the same upper room where the Last Supper took place. There they were surprised by an experience that empowered them to proclaim the gospel. It was, they said, as if a fire fell on them and filled them. Like Easter, Pentecost is a day for baptisms[4] and a day to celebrate the Holy Spirit who renews and strengthens Christians for ministry. To represent the fire of the Spirit, Pentecost is also the one Sunday of the Christian year when the vestments and hangings are always red.

The time after Pentecost is the "long green" season of the church year. The lessons resume the readings that began in

---

4. For many centuries, Pentecost was known in the English-speaking world as Whitsunday (White Sunday) because, though the vestments were red, candidates for baptism were dressed in white.

Epiphany and follow through whichever Gospel is appointed for the particular year. It is a time without the drama of the other seasons, but life is like that. Most of our time is "ordinary time" and a Gospel that fails to strengthen and guide us in the usual days of our lives is less than adequate to our need.

## SAINTS' DAYS

Even before the church had completed the creation of these seasons, it had begun to sprinkle other saints' days and holy days throughout the calendar. If Christmas was to be celebrated on December 25, then nine months before (March 25) was an obvious time to celebrate the angel's visit to Mary to tell her she was to bear the Messiah. Eight days after Christmas was a time to commemorate Jesus' circumcision according to Jewish custom. Other special feasts were the day when Jesus was taken to the temple as an infant (the Presentation, February 2) and the day when he was transfigured on the mountaintop (Transfiguration, August 6; also celebrated, as noted, on the last Sunday after Epiphany). Very early on, the church also began to celebrate the days when members of the church had died for their faith, the "birthday" of their new and eternal life. Most of the apostles were remembered in this way, and then, in later years, other witnesses to the faith were celebrated as well. At first only martyrs were singled out, but eventually other outstanding Christians also were honored. By the time of the Reformation in the sixteenth century, the Christian calendar had become filled up with days commemorating both great saints and those of merely local interest. The reformers, believing that attention paid to the saints and, especially, the Virgin Mary, had begun to diminish the central importance of Christ as "our only Mediator and Advocate" (Prayer Book, page 330), cleared away almost all these celebrations. The Book of Common Prayer at first kept only the days that were directly connected to the New Testament. Other saints, however, continued to be remembered in the names of churches, and All Saints' Day on November 1 remained a time to honor other witnesses. Gradually, and almost inevitably, the need to take note of the witness of especially remarkable Christians has reasserted itself. The Book of Common Prayer now assigns the memory of many such individuals to various days throughout the year. Some were martyrs, some were teachers, some were bishops or priests, and some were deacons and lay people. Some made their witness in the very early days of the church and some in very recent times. The "Martyrs of Memphis," for example, were members of the Community of St. Mary, an order of nuns, some of whom died ministering to the people of Memphis, Tennessee, during a yellow fever epidemic in 1878. Others are J. O. S. Huntington, the founder of the Order of the Holy Cross, a monastic order for men; Jonathan Daniels, an Episcopal seminarian who died in Selma, Alabama, in the civil rights campaigns of the 1960s; and Elizabeth Cady Stanton, who was a campaigner for women's rights. Their names and many others can be found in the front of the Prayer Book, and more information is available in a Prayer Book supplement called "Lesser Feasts and Fasts." Their presence in the calendar reminds us of the various ways in which God calls us to serve, and of the good examples set by people in times and places not far from our own.

The Episcopal Church does not canonize saints as the Roman Catholic Church does. Episcopalians do not believe the church makes saints; God does. All we can do is recognize those who seem special to us for various reasons. The Episcopal Church does that by voting to add other names to the Prayer Book calendar at the General Convention, held once every three years.

The value of the church's calendar is best summed up in the words of a hymn (Hymnal 317):

Feast after feast thus comes and passes by
yet, passing, points to the glad feast above,
giving us foretaste of the festal joy,
the Lamb's great marriage feast of bliss and love.

QUESTIONS FOR FURTHER
THOUGHT AND DISCUSSION

1.  When you were a child, did your church or family practice
any particular traditions in conjunction with seasons in the
church year, such as Advent, Christmas, or Easter? Which were
your favorites? Why? Are you continuing any of those same
traditions today?

2.  During Lent, many Christians abstain from certain foods
and luxuries as a form of self-discipline and sacrifice. As the
author points out, though, "giving up" luxuries for Lent has
been downplayed recently in favor of prayer and charitable
works. What do you believe are the most helpful ways for you
to observe Lent?

3.  The author describes the wise men as symbolizing "the
coming of all nations to worship Christ." Had you considered
this symbolism before? What do you think it means, exactly, in
today's pluralistic society?

4.  Which of the various activities of Holy Week have been
or perhaps will be the most significant in helping you prepare
for and appreciate the full meaning of Easter? Why?

5.  The Book of Common Prayer assigns the memory of
"especially remarkable" Christians to various days throughout
the year. Review the calendar in the BCP, pp. 19–30. Are any
of the names familiar to you? Do others intrigue you? Select a
few individuals to look up in the Prayer Book supplement
"Lesser Feasts and Fasts" and discuss their contributions to the
church.

# The Word

This section of the book will guide you through a typical Prayer Book service of the Holy Eucharist. For the newcomer, every part of the church service may be a surprise, but the Prayer Book service is carefully planned and quite predictable. A writer of detective stories aims to keep us in suspense; later, rereading such a story, we may see how much we missed the first time. In the liturgy also, we will undoubtedly miss a good deal the first time through, but the liturgy is not designed to keep us guessing or hide information from us. The more we know in advance, the less likely we are to miss something and the more likely it is that we can pay attention to all the details. It is when we already know the story that we can enter deeply into its meaning. All the same, even after taking part in the Eucharist for many years, we will continue to come across new insights and find elements we had missed before.

First, as we did with the church building in chapter one, let's step back and look at the over-all shape of the service. The basic "floor plan" is very simple: part one is centered on the Word and part two is centered on the Sacrament. It might be even simpler to say that both parts have to do with the word of God but that in part one, God's word comes to us in spoken form, while in part two, God's Word comes to us in the form of bread and wine. To dramatize this difference, the first part of the service is often centered on the pulpit or on the Bible, while the second part is centered on the altar. Each of these two parts has a number of separate sections that we will look at in order.

The service also includes intercession, or prayers for others, and a general confession of sins.

These usually come between the service of the word and the service of the altar. The confession, however, is sometimes placed at the beginning of the service, especially in Lent to emphasize the penitential nature of the season.

## THE WORD OF GOD

The first part of the service centers on readings from the Bible and a sermon that relates these readings to our daily lives. Before and after the readings are prayers and hymns with the same general theme as the Bible readings. This part of the service comes to a logical conclusion with the Creed. We respond to what we have heard by saying, "We believe . . ." With that quick introduction, let's start once again from the outside and come into the church as we would on a Sunday morning.

## ENTERING THE CHURCH

When you enter the church, you will almost certainly be welcomed by an usher who will hand you a program. A great deal of thought goes into these programs or bulletins, but they can still be difficult for a newcomer to follow. The primary parts of the service are listed, along with instructions on where to find them in the Prayer Book or Hymnal. There is also usually some indication of whether the congregation should stand, sit, or kneel. If you have time before the service, you may find reviewing this information helpful, but it may be easier simply to see what others are doing and follow their example.

You will probably notice that some people stop before entering the pews and bow slightly or *genuflect*—kneel briefly on one knee. People make these gestures of respect toward the cross on the altar or because a sanctuary light (often a hanging candle) indicates that consecrated bread and wine are kept in a tabernacle on or near the altar. Bowing and genuflecting are appropriate ways to recognize that the church is a sacred space in which God is present with us in a special way, but these respectful gestures are optional. Customs vary widely from one church to another, and even within a particular parish, and individuals are free to use them or not as seems appropriate to them.

You will also notice that many church members kneel in prayer for a while after finding their place. They find it helpful—and you may also—to begin with a private word with God. Perhaps you want to offer special needs, or perhaps you simply want to ask God to help you participate in the service as fully as possible. Most people probably speak to God in their own words or take advantage of the time to be silent in God's presence. We are making a transition from the distractions of the world around us to this place of peace. Some also find it helpful to read one or two of the psalms from the Book of Common Prayer. Psalms 23, 42, 43, 100, and 150 are among those that may help you turn your thoughts toward God and the offering of worship. It is enough to sit quietly and let the atmosphere of the church soak in. Members of the congregation may whisper or smile a quick greeting to friends nearby, but they will try not to disturb others who are coming in and who are hoping to use the time to prepare quietly for worship.

## BEGINNING WITH MUSIC

When you come into church before the main service on Sunday morning, organ music often is already being played. This peaceful prelude helps us to make the transition from the abrasive sounds of the outside world to the quieter and more reflective tones of worship. Some churches choose more contemporary music, making less of a contrast with the music that surrounds us all week, in the hope that some will be attracted to a musical style more familiar to them. Either way, music creates a mood, engages our emotions and feelings, and prepares us to move into the acts of worship that follow. The introductory music, or prelude, ends when the service is scheduled to begin, and is usually followed immediately by an opening hymn.

### ANOTHER WORD ABOUT MUSIC

The Episcopal Church gives enormous importance to its music. It is probably (for better or worse!) the only church that provides a separate prayer book and hymnal for use in its services and expects its members to be able to move back and forth between them frequently. Some churches try to overcome the difficulty of juggling by providing the entire text of the service in the bulletin, so that worshipers only need to look up the hymns. Other churches even print the hymns in the bulletin. But most worshipers need to become familiar with both books and be aware that the hymnal has two major sections, one for hymns and one for service music. When you see a number in your bulletin with an "S" in front of it (S–146, for example) you will know that it is service music and can be found in the front of the hymnal. Most churches use only a few sets of service music, and parishioners quickly become familiar with them and don't need to look them up.

Why do we sing? First of all, because music expresses and enhances feelings of joy. The Taliban banned music in

Afghanistan and Puritanical Christians have also prohibited its use, but most religions include music as an essential aspect of the human response to God. Music has enormous power to unite. It is hard to speak a prayer in unison but much easier to sing a hymn in unison. And the sound of music carries better. When the clergy sing or intone a prayer, the words are more easily heard in a large building.

The Episcopal Church draws on a rich treasury for its music, ranging from the plainsong of the early church, the chorale tunes and Scottish psalm tunes of the Reformation, to the African-American spirituals, Appalachian folk songs, and the Native American tunes of the church in this country. In our own day there has been an explosion of new music and texts, and at least two supplemental hymnals are in use in many churches. There is a limit, of course, to the number of hymns that any one congregation can learn, but those used most often will gradually become familiar to the members. The musical gifts God has given us vary widely, but most of us sing in the shower or join in a chorus of "Happy Birthday" for a family celebration—and most of us can contribute, however modestly, to the singing in church. As one hymn asks, "When Christ is Lord of heaven and earth, how can I keep from singing?"

## BEGINNING THE SERVICE

Although the congregation assembles informally, filtering in a few at a time, kneeling for a prayer, sitting quietly and waiting, those who lead the service most often enter in a formal procession. The organist brings the prelude to an end and begins the opening hymn. The congregation stands as the organist plays through the hymn once before the singing begins, and the choir and clergy enter in a formal procession led by acolytes carrying a cross and candles. Sometimes the procession is led by someone carrying a staff or includes a person swinging incense. Acolytes are members of the congregation (often young) who do such things as carry torches and crosses and assist the clergy at the altar at important points in the service. Carrying a staff is an ancient custom that survives in some places. A staff of office was carried before important dignitaries, and so in churches that have one a verger, a volunteer or staff person who cares for the building, or the sexton, the parish custodian, may carry it before the cross on important occasions. Incense was used in Christian services from the earliest times as a way of honoring God. In a day of open sewers and few baths, a sweet smell was very welcome. In our own day, aroma therapy has made us aware again of how odors can enhance our lives.

The opening procession, however it is formed, serves a purely functional purpose: to get people where they need to be to conduct the service. But choir processions are a relatively modern invention and are not required by the Prayer Book. Before the Reformation, choirs were usually made up of monks and were an ordinary part of services in cathedrals and abbeys but not parish churches. After the Reformation, village choirs began to be formed, but they were usually in a gallery at the back of the church and had no reason to wear vestments since they were out of sight. Only with the nineteenth-century Gothic revival were churches built like cathedrals with choir sections at the front, and only then did a choir procession become a useful way of getting the choir where it needed to be.

For a while in the late nineteenth and early twentieth centuries, vested choirs, crosses, torches, and processions were surprisingly controversial. Opponents maintained that it was "Romish" to have such things, although, in fact, the Roman Catholic Church of the time did not have processions or choirs in vestments either. Actually, it makes more sense to locate the choir at the back of the church, and to have the members come in and take their places before the service starts. A choir can sing better in place than while walking, and a choir in a balcony at the back can support congregational singing better than a choir at the front. But choir processions are now so common that it can be very controversial to suggest any other way of beginning the service.

Processions may or may not be useful, but they are not necessary. An opening hymn is not required either, but it can help set the tone of the day and provide a way of turning the individuals who have arrived for the service into a united congregation. Some people bow their heads as the cross is carried past: again, a simple sign of reverence.

ALTERNATIVE BEGINNINGS

There is more than one way to begin a service in the Episcopal Church. For many years, the opening hymn, however exuberant, was always followed by relatively quiet prayers. The priest said a quiet prayer standing before the altar, turned to the congregation, and said the Ten Commandments or the Summary of the Law, and then said or sang the words, "Lord, have mercy upon us; Christ, have mercy upon us; Lord, have mercy upon us." The tone was one of reverence and penitence for sins. Such an opening carried on the pre-Reformation tradition of a heavy emphasis on sin and the need for forgiveness. The Book of Common Prayer allows various approaches, and this kind of opening remains possible. Some parishes still begin the service this way, especially in Lent.

Modern scholars have rediscovered the joyous mood that characterized the worship of the early church, and more churches are now encouraging this spirit. The Book of Common Prayer officially adopted in 1979 made it possible to begin on a note of praise and thankfulness, and this is increasingly common.

The Book of Common Prayer provides for two orders of service. The 1979 edition of the Prayer Book took the radical step of providing prayers and services in contemporary English, but also provided some services in the traditional Elizabethan English for those who preferred something closer to the service they had always known. The contrast between a penitential and joyful emphasis is also reflected in these two forms of service, known as Rite I (the older language and more penitential emphasis) and Rite II (more contemporary in language and more joyful in emphasis). The usual beginning of Rite I can be found in the Prayer Book on page 323 and for Rite II on page 355. Sometimes, especially in Lent, a Penitential Order is used, and the service then begins on page 319 (Rite I) or page 351 (Rite II). In the following sections, numbers in parentheses refer to pages in the Book of Common Prayer.

## THE SALUTATION (323/355)[5]

Remember that there are two focal points at the front of the church: the altar and the pulpit. Since the first part of the service focuses on the proclamation of God's Word, the clergy end the opening procession closer to the pulpit than to the altar. Often they take seats near the choir while the lessons are read.

When in place, the priest begins by greeting the congregation with the words, "Blessed be God: Father, Son, and Holy Spirit," to which the congregation responds, "And blessed be his kingdom, now and for ever. Amen." From the very outset, it is clear that the liturgy is not a performance by the clergy for the people but a dialogue—or, better yet, a trialogue since the

---

5. Numbers in parentheses throughout the rest of this book refer to page numbers in the Book of Common Prayer.

conversation is with God as well—in which clergy and congregation both have important parts to play.

## COLLECT FOR PURITY AND HYMN OF PRAISE (323/355)

After this exchange of greetings there are several options. These variations make it more difficult for newcomers, but the possibility of choices allows the service to reflect the changing moods of different church seasons. In Rite I, and often in Rite II, what follows the greeting is a very beautiful prayer called the Collect for Purity that has a long history of use in the Anglican Communion. It asks God, who knows the secrets of our hearts, to cleanse and purify them so we may worthily offer God our praise. Rite I, shaped to reflect the medieval penitential tradition, makes the greeting optional and the collect mandatory. Rite II, seeking to recover the joyous worship of the early church, does just the opposite, making the greeting mandatory and the collect optional.

Rite I continues in a penitential mood by offering the option of reciting the Ten Commandments or the Summary of the Law. In Rite II it's possible to proceed directly from the greeting to the song of the angels, "Glory to God in the highest" (356), or some other song of praise. The whole congregation may sing this hymn to a familiar tune or the choir may perform a more elaborate version, or the congregation may say it in unison, depending on the size of the congregation and the musical resources available.

Although the *Gloria* is prescribed for the most joyous seasons of the year, it is not used in Advent or Lent. Two alternative hymns are provided for use at other times. Since they are used especially in the penitential seasons we often assume that they are penitential themselves, but it would be better to see them instead as simply less joyful than the Gloria. The first alternative, "Lord, have mercy," (356) known as the *Kyrie* from its first word in Greek, may sound to modern ears like a plea for forgiveness, but it was originally a shout of praise used in the presence of the emperor. In the same way, the English shout "God save the Queen (or King)" not as a plea for help but as a kind of cheer or shout of praise. The second alternative, the *Trisagion* ("Holy God, Holy and Mighty, Holy Immortal One, Have mercy upon us," page 356) is a traditional hymn of praise in the Eastern Church.

Each of these three hymns goes back to the fourth century or earlier. It is significant that the "Lord, have mercy" may also be sung in Greek. It was so familiar so early that even in the Latin mass it is still said or sung in Greek. Using it in that language unites us with Christians in every century who have always sung it in that form.

## THE COLLECT OF THE DAY (325/357)

When we come to the next prayer, we set the theme of the day directly. We have talked about the seasons of the year and how they came into existence with the two focal points of Easter and Christmas. These two seasons, with their preparatory seasons of Lent and Advent, apparently took shape by the fourth or fifth centuries so that each Sunday in these seasons had its own special prayer and selected Bible readings. It took a much longer time to provide a special set of readings and prayers for the remaining Sundays after Epiphany and Pentecost. We take it for granted that each Sunday should have different readings and prayers, and it is an understandable instinct. Traditions of this sort seem to have been present in pre-Christian Judaism. Nevertheless, for many centuries, the ordinary Sundays were left without specific assignment. In some evangelical churches even today there are no such traditions: the clergy are free to choose whatever readings they wish and to compose prayers for the occasion as the Spirit moves them.

It is part of the Anglican tradition, however, to assign a specific prayer and readings for every Sunday and holy day. These special prayers are called "Collects," because we "collect" our thoughts around a particular theme. Many of these prayers are very old and reflect the chaotic years of the early Middle Ages when asking for peaceful times and protection against enemies was a priority. Newer Collects tend to ask more generally for gifts of faith and love. The Collect is preceded by the priest saying: "The Lord be with you." The congregation responds: "And with thy spirit" (325), or "And also with you" (357).

The typical Collect has a very definite form with three parts. First is an address to God, speaking of some aspect of God's character:

"O God, you declare your almighty power chiefly in showing mercy and pity . . ."
"O God, who made this holy night to shine with the glory of the Lord's resurrection . . ."
"O God, you make us glad by the yearly festival of the birth of your only Son . . ."

This is followed by a petition:

"Grant that this light . . . may shine forth in our lives . . .,"
"Mercifully hear the supplications of your people . . ."
"Give us grace to heed [the prophets'] warnings . . ."

And finally, the closing asks that what we have requested may be granted "through Jesus Christ our Lord." The ending usually has a Trinitarian form, reminding us that Jesus Christ "lives and reigns with you [God] and the Holy Spirit, one God," and that this is eternally true: "for ever and ever."

Most of the Collects in ordinary time have no specific connection to the readings, but some of them have become so well
known that they give a special character to their Sunday.
"Blessed Lord, who hast caused all holy Scripture to be written
for our learning . . ." (184/236) for example, marked the Second Sunday in Advent as "Scripture Sunday" for many years.
Now transferred to a Sunday in November, it has yet to make
its mark on the new date. Likewise, the Collect that began
with the words "Stir up . . ." (160/212) once came on the fifth
Sunday before Christmas and reminded housewives of the
need to stir up the Christmas pudding. In the age of instant
everything, the words have been moved to only two weeks
before Christmas.

Many of the Collects repay close study because of their
carefully balanced phrases and precisely chosen words. Notice
for example, how the Collect for the first Sunday in Advent
(159/211) balances light and dark, mortal and immortal life,
humility and majesty, now and on the last day. Thomas Cran-
mer, the Archbishop of Canterbury who was chiefly responsible for the first English Prayer Book, is noted most of all for his
work translating and composing the Collects. He has been
compared to someone setting words in place as a jeweler sets
precious stones. Since many parishes provide the Collect and
readings on an insert in the Sunday bulletin, it would be easy
to take it along for daily reading during the week. These are
prayers that will richly reward you for such continued use and
meditation.

## READING THE SCRIPTURES
### BACKGROUND

Sometime in the middle of the second century, about a
hundred years after the Resurrection, a man called Justin
described the way worship took place in his community. "On

the day of the sun," he wrote, "we assemble . . . and the mem-
oirs of the apostles are read as long as time permits."[6] There's a
wonderful sense of freedom and informality in his picture of
Christian worship. You can almost imagine the reader stopping
to ask whether anyone was feeling pushed for time or whether
he could go on a while longer.

With time, of course, Christians would begin to feel that
they wanted to hear certain portions of Scripture read at certain times. On the anniversary of Jesus' resurrection, they
would want to hear those stories again. In the weeks before
Easter, they would want to hear again of Jesus' last journey to
Jerusalem, the prophecies behind these events, and the letters
of Paul and others that interpreted what had happened. Gradually it became customary to read the Scriptures in a fixed pattern. By the fifth and sixth centuries, churches throughout
western Europe were following very similar calendars govern-
ing what was read and when. For Anglicans, Lutherans, and
many others, the Reformation did not change much in this
calendar. On the fourth Sunday of Lent, Christians who followed the liturgical year read of the feeding of the five thousand and on the first Sunday in Advent they read of the entry
of Jesus into Jerusalem. Each Sunday of the year had readings
assigned to it, and those readings became very familiar while
the rest of the Bible remained largely unknown.

Then, in the last half of the twentieth century, something
unprecedented happened: a group of experts sat down to plan
a new calendar that revolutionized the way Scripture was read
in church. For the first time ever, there would be a three-year
cycle of readings—nearly three times as much Scripture was to
be read—and the readings would provide continuity from week
to week. When the Episcopal Church adopted the current

6 Justin, *Apology* I.lxv-lxviii.

Prayer Book in 1979, this new calendar of readings, called a *lectionary*, was adopted and placed in the back of the Prayer Book (889–931).

As time went on, people felt a need to revise this lectionary in some respects. Eventually, an ecumenical committee produced the "Revised Common Lectionary," and the General Convention authorized its use on an experimental basis beginning in 2002. As a result, not all Episcopal churches now read the same lessons on Sunday since some have adopted the new schedule and some have not. The differences are not major—they apply mostly to Old Testament lessons read after Pentecost—and the shape of the lectionary remains largely the same. For churches using either version of the Common Lectionary, the three-year cycle concentrates on the Gospel according to Matthew in the first year (Year A), the Gospel according to Mark in the second year (Year B), and the Gospel according to Luke in the third year (Year C). The Gospel of John is not neglected but added at appropriate points, especially in Lent. In a similar way, the Epistles are read through in se-quence. First Corinthians, for example, is read in Epiphany and the Epistle to the Romans is read in the Sundays after Pentecost in Year A. The story of the early church in Acts, and the vision of the end of time in Revelation are read during the Easter season. Perhaps the most important change made in the Revised Common Lectionary is that the Old Testament can now be read in sequence, especially in the season after Pentecost. The first books of the Bible, Genesis and Exodus, are read in Year A, while the history books, 1 and 2 Samuel and 1 and 2 Kings are read in Years B and C. It's amazing to think of it in these terms, but beginning in this twenty-first century, the major Christian churches are being exposed to more Scripture more systematically than ever before.

OLD TESTAMENT, PSALM, EPISTLE, GOSPEL

Now, what happens on Sunday morning when the lectionary comes to life? We have moved through the introductory parts of the service, standing for the opening hymn and salutation, we have said or sung the Gloria, Kyrie, or Trisagion, and we have offered in prayer the Collect for the Day. After that, the congregation sits down and someone, most often a member of the congregation, goes to a reading desk called the lectern to read the first appointed passage of Scripture. Almost always this first reading comes from the Old Testament. Some parishes choose to omit the Old Testament and read only two lessons instead of three. In Easter the first reading may be from the Acts of the Apostles, but normally we begin with the Old Testament background, the story of how God's people were led through the long centuries that prepared them for the coming of the Messiah. At the end of the reading, the lector (the person reading the lesson) may say: "The Word of the Lord." The congregation responds: "Thanks be to God" (325/357).

Whatever the reading may be, no matter how often we have heard it, and regardless of our education level, we all need time to ponder and digest what we have heard. We are in a different situation this year than when we listened to it three years ago, and the same Scripture may speak to us now in new ways. Usually there's a time of silence after the reading to give us the opportunity to consider what we have heard. The time provided will almost certainly not be enough. Perhaps the best we can do with the brief time allotted is to think back (or look back if printed copies of the reading are provided) and find a few words we can reflect on later in the day.

After the time of silence, we come to the one book of the Bible that is normally read at every service, the Book of Psalms. The psalms have been the hymns of God's people for well over two thousand years. They reflect every mood from joy to despair and provide us with the words we need more reliably than any other book.

The Psalter is different from the rest of the Bible in another way: it is not read to us, but instead we all participate in the reading. There are many different ways of participating. Sometimes we read the psalm responsively, sometimes we sing it, and sometimes the choir sings it while the congregation sings an antiphon or refrain after each group of two or three verses. It is, after all, a hymnal, and though the poetry is different from the kind of rhymed verses we are familiar with in the hymnal, it is poetry and so it speaks to us in a different way than prose: it suggests, it appeals to our emotions, its words and phrases stay with us and repeat themselves in our minds.

The psalm also serves as a kind of buffer between the readings. We can't absorb three Bible readings in a row without a break. The psalm provides that change of pace, and by speaking to the same theme in different words, it may provide another way to meditate on the Scripture passage we have heard.

When we have said or sung the psalm, there is a second reading from Scripture, this time from the New Testament. Again, a member of the congregation (though sometimes one of the clergy) goes to a lectern to read the appointed passage, usually one of the Epistles. These are letters written by St. Paul and other early church leaders to congregations just beginning to understand the meaning of the gospel. Our world may be very different, but the problems we encounter are often very similar. What, for example, is the meaning of baptism? What do we mean when we talk about the Resurrection? What do we mean by "faith" and "grace"? How can we resolve the matter if some members of the congregation want to keep rules that others say we can ignore? In addition to these and other practical questions, there are the great passages about love (1 Corinthians 13) and faith (Hebrews 11) and the imitation of Christ (Philippians 2:5–11). The Epistle is not simply a letter to the early church, it is a letter to us. At the conclusion of the reading, the lector may again say: "The Word of the Lord," and the congregation responds: "Thanks be to God." As with the Old Testament, this reading is usually followed by a period of silence so that we can think about what we have heard and what it might mean for us.

Once again, the lesson is usually followed by a hymn. In the Middle Ages, worshipers chanted a verse of Scripture preceded and followed by "Alleluias," while a special Gospel book was carried to the place where it would be read. These verses were called *sequences.* They were often sung by a single voice and became increasingly elaborate. In the late Middle Ages in northern Europe, a new type of chant with words that rhymed became popular. Eventually rhyming chant evolved into the kind of hymns we sing today. Some parishes still sing the ancient sequences, but generally congregations sing modern hymns. Sometimes the choir sings an anthem at this point. Whatever style of hymn is used in a particular congregation, the purpose is always the same: to provide another opportunity to reflect on the words of Scripture just heard and to throw new light on them. The hymn may be as general as a simple expression of praise or as specific as a paraphrase of the Epistle or Gospel. It may also be chosen because its theme is closely related to the Gospel that will be read as soon as the hymn is over.

Whether the words of the hymn move in the direction of the Gospel or not, attention does begin to shift toward the Gospel during this hymn. It is very common practice today to have a "Gospel procession" during which the Gospel book is carried to some prominent place before it is read. This procession may come down the aisle to the center of the congregation or go to the pulpit. It may be very elaborate, with acolytes carrying a cross and torches and even using incense. Or, on the other hand, it may be very simple: the deacon or priest carrying the book alone to the place where it will be read. The congregation stands (if they have not been standing already for a hymn) and turns toward the place where the Gospel is being read. The Gospel is the story of what Jesus did and said, and it is a long-established custom to treat the reading as if Christ himself were with us. We stand to honor him.

Before the Gospel lesson is read the reader says to the congregation: "The Holy Gospel of our Lord Jesus Christ according to . . ." with the name of the day's Gospel writer inserted. The congregation responds: "Glory be to thee, O Lord," in Rite I (326) or "Glory to you, Lord Christ," in Rite II (357). At the conclusion of the reading, the lector declares: "The Gospel of the Lord," and the congregation responds "Praise be to thee, O Christ," in Rite I, and "Praise to you, Lord Christ," in Rite II.

The reading of the Gospel is the climax of the first part of the Eucharist. In it the Word of God comes to us and Christ speaks to us. But we ask, "What does that mean to me?" The sermon, which follows the Gospel immediately, is intended to respond to that very natural question. There was a day—it is still true in some churches—when the sermon was the high point of the service and the most important work of the clergy. Sermons routinely lasted an hour or more, and families discussed them in detail over the dining table. Modern Americans, barraged with information of every sort, are often overloaded with information and unable to absorb any more. We are accustomed to getting information in short bursts and sound bites, but have much less experience paying close attention to a spoken presentation, especially if it lacks the special effects of television or movies. No wonder sermons are shorter

and receive less attention. But clergy are still called and ordained not only to be pastors and administrators of the sacraments, but also to proclaim the Word of God, and God does
speak through today's sermons. Just as God's presence in the
sacrament does not depend on the quality of the bread, so the
Word of God in the sermon does not depend on the oratorical
skills of the preacher or the analytical skills of the listener.
Careful preparation of a sermon and attentive listening will, of
course, be rewarded, but God often speaks through the sermon
in ways neither the preacher nor hearer expected. A seed may
be sown that bears fruit at some later date. The Word of God is
not limited by our human weakness.

## THE CREED (326/358)

As we have said, we are given opportunity to respond to
each of the lessons read aloud. After the sermon, however, the
response is different. We are responding now to all the readings
and the sermon, and our response is the traditional statement
of faith called the Nicene Creed, which we stand and recite in
unison.

The Creed began as a simple statement of faith made by
those being baptized. In that shorter form, it is still used today
in the baptismal service. When controversy over the nature of
Christ broke out in the fourth century, a council was called to
resolve the issue. This council met in the year 325 at Nicaea, a
town near the present capital of Turkey, Istanbul. Bishops
came from all over the Mediterranean world for the first such
gathering ever. After a long and passionate debate, they adopted
an expanded version of the baptismal creed, which became
known as the Nicene Creed. It was somewhat revised at subse-
quent councils over the next hundred and twenty-five years,
although Christians did not begin using it as part of the service
until several centuries later.

There is a difference between worship and theology. In worship, we are not usually stating our belief, but rather acting it out. It is worth remembering, however, that our faith does have a clear and specific content. We know what we believe and, having heard it read and expounded, it is appropriate to affirm our commitment to the Gospel by reciting the Creed.

## THE PRAYERS

What happens next is not an essential element of the Eucharist, though it is an important part of any Christian life. Part of our ministry as members of the church is to pray for others. Part of our growth as Christians comes when we confess our sins. *Intercession,* our prayers for others, and *confession* are important aspects of Christian living; it is appropriate to include them between the two main parts of the service.

Christians should and do pray for each other often. St. Paul, in his letters to the early Christian churches, speaks frequently of his prayers for them and asks them to pray for him. It is natural for Christians to pray both privately and when they come together. It is also natural that these prayers should come from many voices, since no one person knows the needs of all the various members. Early in the life of the church deacons were responsible for the church's ministry to those in need and were more aware of those who needed prayers than the priest. If there is a deacon in the parish, intercession is still the deacon's usual responsibility, but since the intercession is "the Prayers of the People," it is also commonly led by lay members of the congregation. Whoever leads the prayer, members of the congregation always have the opportunity to add prayers for individuals and causes of concern to them, and to offer thanksgiving as well. Slowly, Episcopalians are becoming accustomed to speaking their own individual prayers out loud.

The Prayer Book provides seven alternative forms for our intercessions, one in Rite I (328–330) and six more in Rite II. Any of these alternatives may be used with either service. For many centuries, the Prayer Book communion service provided only one form of intercession, and it was a long prayer said by the priest with only an "Amen" from the congregation at the end. This response pattern is still provided by the Intercession in Rite I, though the congregation may now be invited to respond to each specific petition. Members of modern congregations are unaccustomed to absorbing longer statements than sound bites, and it is important that they have frequent opportunities to respond and stay involved. All the other forms of intercession provide this opportunity.

It is worthwhile to take a closer look at these prayers because they come from a wide variety of sources and reflect different ways of looking at the needs of the world. The forms provided for Rite II are at the end of the service (383–393). Forms I and V are based on forms used in the Orthodox Church that go back to the very early church and are associated with Sts. Basil and Chrysostom. Forms II and VI, on the other hand, were composed by Episcopal clergy in the twentieth century. Form III is drawn from the new Prayer Book of the Church in New Zealand. Form IV began with the Church of England in the twentieth century but was revised by the Church of South Africa before being revised again for use in the American Prayer Book. The Prayer Book has always drawn from a wide variety of historical sources, but now it draws on a variety of geographical sources as well.

All the intercessions include prayers "for those in positions of public trust." These prayers are part of the "establishment" heritage of the Episcopal Church and that has sometimes caused severe problems. At the time of the American Revolution, Anglican clergy had to decide whether to pray for King

George III and all the royal family or to break their ordination oath of loyalty to the Prayer Book. When the war was over and a new American Prayer Book was created, it was quite natural for the Episcopal Church to insert prayers for the president instead. Today, because of that heritage, the Episcopal Church is unique in its insistence on praying for the government at almost every service. On the other hand, the Prayer Book seems not to acknowledge fully the transition from monarchy to a republic; most of its prayers speak only of the president and not the other co-equal branches of government. Some of those leading these prayers correct that deficiency by adding (as the Prayer Book allows them to do) "the Congress and the Courts." It is worth noticing that prayers for the environment and natural order did not become part of our service until the publication of the 1979 Prayer Book. Now we also pray for those who travel by air and in outer space. These were not concerns of the church even one century ago. More controversial until recent times were prayer for the faithful departed and prayer commemorating the saints. The Reformers of the sixteenth century opposed such prayers, largely because the practice had been grossly abused. The sale of "indulgences," said to free the dead from purgatory, triggered Martin Luther's opposition to the medieval Roman Church. Most Protestant churches still do not give thanks for the saints or pray for the dead. The Episcopal Church reclaimed this ancient tradition with the 1928 edition of the Prayer Book, and the current Prayer Book takes it for granted that when those we love die, their deaths should be no barrier to our prayers for them.

## THE CONFESSION AND ABSOLUTION

There was a time in the early days of the church when Christians not only stated their intercessions, but also confessed their own particular sins. Some evangelical churches

today still follow this custom, but Episcopalians generally are
not yet ready to go that far. Nevertheless, the confession of sin
that usually occurs at this point ought to be thought of as a
general statement of our own particular failures. In saying the
general words, "We have not loved our neighbors as ourselves,"
for example, we should keep in mind that our neighbor was
sick and we failed to call or offer help, that our neighbor (in
global terms) was hungry, exiled, imprisoned, dying, and we
failed to raise our pledge or contribute to the appeal made in
the parish newsletter. It is easy to join thoughtlessly in a general confession. The absolution that follows can hardly absolve
us of sins we have failed to confess or even consider our own.

In the Middle Ages people ordinarily received communion
only once a year, and then only after making a private confession of sin to a priest. The Reformation set out to change this
pattern, by including confession in the service. Even so, it was
not expected that people would come to communion in large
numbers. Those who did receive communion came forward
during the service and knelt around the altar. The invitation to
the Confession in Rite I still reflects that practice in the words
"draw near with faith," which were said when members moved
up to kneel around the altar. The Rite I (330) invitation spells
out the requirements for a good confession: that we "truly and
earnestly repent . . . and are in love and charity with [our]
neighbors, and intend to lead a new life." The Rite II invitation asks only that we "confess our sins against God and our
neighbor" (360), but the Confession itself asks us to say that
we "are truly sorry and . . . humbly repent" and asks help so
that we may in the future "walk in [God's] ways." "On occasion," the Confession may be omitted, but since a primary
purpose of the Eucharist is to help us be reconciled with God
and our neighbors, it remains a valuable part of the regular service. Before coming to church, many church members prepare

for this part of the service by examining their consciences and asking God's forgiveness.

## THE PEACE

The logical sequence of the service brings us now to a ceremony called *the Peace* (332/360). For Episcopalians, the informal exchange of greetings at a formal service is a rather new thing. Some still find it difficult and out of character, but it is a very ancient ceremony with roots in Judaism. The early Christians took it for granted as a symbol of unity and quickly made it part of their services. Jesus once rebuked a host for failing to offer him a kiss when he arrived for a meal, and he instructed his disciples not to approach the altar if they were not reconciled with their brothers and sisters. The earliest document recording Christian Eucharistic prayers (the *Didache,* c. a.d. 100) specifically refers to the exchange of a kiss after the prayers and before the offering. The enthusiasm with which this ancient ceremony is enacted varies from one congregation to another. Some members of the congregation may exchange hugs and kisses, especially with family members, while others simply clasp hands. Individuals may repeat the words "The peace of the Lord be always with you" to each other, or "Peace be with you" or simply "Peace" or the Hebrew word "Shalom."

It may be helpful to think of the Peace in terms of a family gathering for Thanksgiving Day. Suppose a family's custom is to come together for an enormous meal and they begin to arrive at the appointed place, from near and far. As they come in, uncles and cousins and grandchildren exchange greetings. If they're a close and warm family, there are hugs and kisses and cries of greeting. If they see each other often, they may just smile and nod or offer a handshake. That's a lot like what happens at the Peace. The members of God's family have come together to share a meal. We may or may not have had a chance to speak to one or two others on the way in, but we aren't likely to have a chance to talk to many. Yet we are a family; more than that, we are members of one body. We cannot gather at God's table like strangers at separate tables in a restaurant. We come because we are united in faith and share one life. A hymn often used at communion compares us to "grain once scattered on the hillside," which is "in this broken bread made one." The Peace is our always-inadequate attempt to express and affirm the joy of that unity before we go to God's table. Individuals and congregations have their own particular styles of greeting, but regardless of the style, if the greeting is done well, it helps create the sense of unity in Christ that lies at the heart of our faith.

This exchange of the Peace has a very specific relationship to the forgiveness in Christ that we have just received and the approach we are about to make to God's altar. It is not an opportunity to discuss the weather or last night's ball game. It is an opportunity to recognize the unity we have in Christ that transcends all the barriers human beings tend to create between themselves. It is a holy and solemn moment—and that does include great joy.

## QUESTIONS FOR FURTHER
## THOUGHT AND DISCUSSION

1.  How important is music to you in taking part in worship? Do you have a preference as to which type—traditional or contemporary—is used in the worship service?

2.  Compare the traditional Collects, beginning on p. 159 of the BCP, with the contemporary, beginning on p. 211, noting especially the difference in the tone and style of the language. Which one helps you achieve a better sense of worship? Why?

3.  Are the Scripture readings helpful to you, or do you feel that you don't fully understand their meanings at times? What could you do to derive more benefit from the readings?

4.  Describe the most memorable sermon you've ever heard and why it meant so much to you.

5.  The author mentions an old controversy about prayer for the "faithful departed" in the section entitled "The Prayers." What value do you find, if any, in praying for the dead?

6.  According to the author, many church members prepare for the Confession element of the service by examining their consciences and asking God's forgiveness. Does the Confession during the service have real meaning for you as a means of finding absolution for your sins? Why or why not?

# The Sacrament

Before we go on to the second part of the service, let's take a quick look back at its history. We could go all the way back to the Jews' captivity in Egypt to examine the great events that set them free. We could talk about the Passover meal eaten with haste on that last night in Egypt, and commemorated every year afterwards by Jewish people everywhere. It was—and is—their "Fourth of July" celebration, a remembrance of the day that celebrates their freedom from slavery. Scholars disagree as to whether the meal Jesus shared with his disciples on the night before he was crucified was on Passover itself or on the evening before the Passover. Either way, Passover was the setting for that final meal, and whenever we celebrate the Eucharist, we relive that ancient story. And we do more than relive it, because that story was given new meaning when Jesus celebrated it with his disciples in Jerusalem just before he died. During that meal, he took break and wine, broke the bread, gave thanks to God for the bread and wine, and gave them to his disciples saying, "This is my body . . . this is my blood." At the moment, they could hardly have understood what he meant, but after he was crucified and rose from the dead, they understood that meal as a celebration of freedom even greater than that from slavery: freedom from sin and from the fear of death. The early Christians understood Jesus' death to be like that of the Passover lamb. Through his death God's people are set free.

If you look carefully at the way all four Gospels tell the story, you will see something odd: the Gospel according to John tells of Jesus teaching his disciples at the Last Supper but never mentions bread and wine; the other three Gospels, Matthew, Mark, and Luke, say little if anything about Jesus teaching that night and simply record the things he did. Clearly both the teaching and the action are important, but it is difficult to concentrate on both at the same time.

For the God of the Bible, word and action are part of one whole. In the first part of the service, we explore the ways in which we act out the words we say. We don't just sit and listen: we stand, we sit, we move, we respond. God acts in our lives to transform them. "The word of God," the Bible tells us, "is living and active, sharper than any two-edged sword" (Hebrews 4:12). Since we have been paying attention to Jesus' teaching in the first part of the service, it makes sense for us to concentrate on the actions in the second part. Through both, through the power of God's active word in both, God is at work transforming and renewing our lives. Christian worship, at its best, balances word and sacrament.

The Prayer Book defines the sacraments as "outward and visible signs of inward and spiritual grace" (857). In other words, sacraments are physical, material signs of the invisible power—the grace of God—at work in our lives. In the Episcopal Church, following an ancient tradition, the two central sacraments are baptism and the Eucharist. Water, in the first case, and bread and wine in the second case, become the means of God's grace. Could God act in us without sacraments? Of

course. But that is like asking whether a parent can love a child
without touching. Theoretically it is possible; under some circumstances it may be the only way to work. But normally we
express ourselves with our bodies and are acted on by other
beings through their bodies. For God to use physical means to
impact our lives is simply the natural way for a Creator to
work in creation. God can work in our lives without sacraments, and some churches are content with that. But why
limit God or ourselves? The Episcopal Church employs a rich
variety of outward signs and actions to aid us in worshiping
God and to show God's love for us. Like any language, the language of sacrament may not always be clear at first, but a little
study and experience can open up new ways through which
God can speak to us—and we can speak to God.

## THE SHAPE OF THE LITURGY

We have spoken of sacraments as "visible signs," the means
by which God speaks to our physical senses of a deeper and
invisible action. The gospel story tells us how Jesus often used
such signs to minister to the people around him: he touched
the eyes of the blind and the ears of the deaf, he provided fish
and bread to satisfy human hunger. In our worship, when we
commemorate the Last Supper, a pattern of actions is critical
to our understanding of the entire service. Jesus took bread,
blessed it, broke it, and gave it to his disciples. Those four
actions were not unfamiliar to his disciples. When Jesus fed the
multitudes with bread and wine, the Gospels tell us that he
also took, blessed, broke, and gave. It seems to have been so
familiar a pattern that, on Easter Day, two disciples walking
away from Jerusalem, sad and discouraged because of Jesus'
death and the failure of their hopes, recognized their risen
Lord only when he sat down with them at a table, took bread,
blessed, broke, and gave it to them (St. Luke 24:30). The

whole second part of the Eucharist is simply an elaboration of those four actions.

## THE OFFERTORY (333/361)

The first of the four actions is the taking of bread and wine. We call it the *Offertory.* It is a movement of great significance, but so much is going on in the service at this time that we can easily miss the point. The sharing of the Peace has just broken the mood of the service with a moment of informality. The Peace is often followed by parish announcements, which also are usually quite informal. The priest usually ends them with a sentence from Scripture known as "The Offertory Sentence," which marks the formal beginning of the next major segment of the service. It is normally said with no great ceremony, so the Offertory Sentence often seems to be only a signal to the ushers to begin taking up the collection. As the ushers carry plates up and down the aisles, the choir may sing an anthem or the congregation may sing a hymn. At the same time, the priest, acolytes, and other assistants may be moving from the choir to the altar, and a small procession may bring bread and wine to the altar, as well as the money offering from the back of the church. There is probably no other point in the service at which so many things are happening simultaneously. But our attention should focus primarily on the bread and wine that are brought to the altar. The Offertory, whatever the name may seem to imply, is not only about money. The Offertory Sentence is an invitation to the whole congregation to join in the action for which we were created: to offer our lives to God in love and worship.

A wonderful poem by James Weldon Johnson called "The Creation" describes God setting out tools and going to work to make a world. In somewhat the same way, the second part of the service begins with a collecting of all the elements so that

God can work in them and through them in us. The priest moves to the altar and ushers come down the aisles gathering the offering. Then the ushers, along with other members of the congregation, move forward to the altar carrying the offering plates and containers of bread and wine. In the early days of the church, members of the congregation brought forward bread and wine they had made, and it was collected at the front of the church. What was needed for the service was placed on the altar, and the rest was set aside for those who were in need. Since few of us make our own bread and wine these days, it's simpler for us to bring money to buy bread and wine for the service, and support the needs of the church and of the less fortunate.

The money, bread, and wine serve a very practical purpose. The bread and wine will be used in the service, and the money will be used to pay the church's bills and to reach out to others. But there is much more to it than that. The bread and wine have been bought with the money we give; they represent the work we have done during the week as surely as the money does. St. Augustine once said of this moment, "There you are upon the altar." It is a stunning image: there I am on the altar in the bread and wine to be offered to the God who made me. The bread taken to the altar is our life, and, amazingly and wonderfully, it will be returned to us as the life of Christ. In this service our life and Christ's life are united, and we go out renewed in his life. Likewise, the money is more than a matter of the church's budget: a significant part of that budget is used to meet the needs of others at home and far away, and to tell others the good news of God's love. Even the cost of the church's heat and light has a missionary impact. Such expenditures maintain the church building, and its existence announces to the world that Christ's ministry is based there.

It is worth remembering that bread and wine are both made as the result of yeast working in a basic foodstuff. Wheat and grapes are natural crops; they grow "wild" in many parts of the world. Over long centuries, human beings may have "improved" them, but they remain a "God-given" part of the world around us. We harvest these crops and process them, adding yeast, which works from within to transform them into bread and wine. What could be a more appropriate symbol of what God is doing through this service: taking human lives and working within us to make us a new people to serve God's purpose?

The music is an offering, too. Whether it's the choir, the congregation, or both who are singing, we sing to offer praise to God, not to demonstrate our musical skills. Through all these actions and elements, we re-live what Jesus did at the Last Supper.

With all the activity involved in the Offertory, it is odd but true that the congregation can sometimes feel a bit left out. If we are people who respond easily and deeply to music, it may be that a choir anthem will lift us out of ourselves and prepare us for the central action of the service. Others, however, may find all the movement a bit distracting, and they may not be caught up in the music in the same way. It is important not to let our minds drift away from the liturgy; we need to find ways to remain involved. Often the words of the anthem can be a focus for our thoughts. If not, the Offertory Sentence, the sermon we have just heard, or the words of one of the hymns may provide the inspiration we need to keep ourselves centered.

## THE GREAT THANKSGIVING (333–336/361–363)

The second thing Jesus did at the Last Supper was to give thanks. At any formal meal, we first prepare the table, and then we give thanks for our food. Just as many Christians say

grace at home around the table, so we do the same thing here
as God's family at God's table. It was customary for Jewish
people to give thanks to God for all food, and especially at the
Passover meal they gave thanks for their deliverance from slavery. So Jesus did at the Last Supper, and so we do today.

It may be a little confusing that sometimes we speak of
"blessing" the food at a meal and sometimes of "giving thanks."
Both terms are used in the Gospel accounts of the Last Supper.
We may find it helpful to think of them as two sides of the
same coin. The word *bless* seems to refer to God's action, and
*give thanks* to ours. Even though we may speak of human
beings "blessing" something, God is the ultimate source of the
blessing. It is not we who bless the food either at home or here.
Rather, we respond to God's blessing by blessing God (or giving thanks to God), and as we do, God blesses the food and
blesses us.

During the Offertory, the deacon or priest places certain
items on the altar. First a square of white cloth called the *corpo-
ral* is spread at the center of the altar. The bread brought to the
altar is then placed on a plate, and the wine is poured into a
cup with a little water. The water may remind us of the blood
and water that flowed from Jesus' side at the crucifixion (John
19:34), but it is also true that water was normally added to
wine in first-century Palestine. The *plate* and *cup* used in the
service may be made of very simple material, but usually are
made of precious metals like silver and gold. After all, they are
to be used to hold the body and blood of Christ, so it is appropriate that they are the very best we can provide. The plate and
cup used in the Eucharist are often called the *paten* and *chalice,*
though the Prayer Book itself does not use these technical
terms. Ideally there will be one cup of wine and one loaf of
bread to symbolize the unity we have through sharing them.
When the bread and wine have been placed in readiness, the

priest may go to the side of the altar to let an acolyte pour water over his or her fingers into a small bowl. This *lavabo* action is symbolic, and reminds us again of the holiness of the occasion. We need to approach God's table not only with clean hands but also with a clean heart. Now the priest may pray silently the words of a psalm, "I will wash my hands in innocence, O Lord, that I may go [to] your altar" (Psalm 26:6 alt.).

When everything has been put in order on the altar, the priest invites the congregation to "lift up" their hearts, to give their whole attention to this central act of worship and praise. The brief dialogue called the *Sursum Corda* ("Lift up your hearts," 333 or 361) is often sung to add special emphasis to it. It continues with a very specific statement of purpose: "Let us give thanks to the Lord our God." The congregation responds, "It is right to give God thanks and praise," and the priest's response emphasizes that it is not only right but "a good and joyful thing, always and everywhere" to give God thanks and praise. (The words vary slightly in Rite I, but convey the same sentiment.) This ancient dialogue between priest and people can be traced to the second century, and it makes it clear that what is about to happen is not the action of the priest alone. The entire congregation joins in the action, though priest and people play different parts.

The Sursum Corda is followed by a brief *Preface* that leads into the main body of the *Prayer of Consecration.* On special occasions the Preface is expanded by a *Proper Preface,* which states the special reason we give thanks at a particular festival or season. Proper Prefaces are also provided for ordinary Sundays, but not for ordinary weekdays. The Book of Common Prayer refers to these Proper Prefaces in italics at the point where they are to be inserted, but it fails to tell us where they may be found. This omission can leave newcomers feeling a little lost as the priest goes on with words that are not on the page. The texts are on pages 344ff. and 377ff., but they are brief, and it may be best just to listen and wait until the priest comes back to the concluding paragraph of the Preface.

The end of the Preface leads into the ancient song called the *Sanctus,* the Latin word for "holy." The words of this song were first recorded by the prophet Isaiah some seven hundred years before the time of Christ. They are found again in the Book of Revelation where St. John describes the worship that takes place in heaven. Bach, Mozart, and other great composers have set the Sanctus to music. Modern versions in both jazz and folk idioms are also available. Most congregations learn one or two musical settings for regular use, but choirs often sing the Sanctus in some of the classic settings at Christmas, Easter, and other times as well.

The Prayer Book directs members of the congregation to stand through the Sursum Corda and Preface, and then states that they may stand or kneel for what follows. Earlier we discussed how the first Christians stood for their prayers, but kneeling became common in the Middle Ages. If the priest and the people remain standing, it is more obvious that they are joined in a common action, but kneeling has a long tradition behind it and is also appropriate. Since the priest usually faces the congregation across the altar, it is worth noticing that the priest dramatizes the words by hand and body movements. The priest's hands may sweep upward in a gesture of offering at the words, "Lift up your hearts," and be held in an open gesture of prayer during much of what follows. The priest may also make the sign of the cross where the words speak of blessing. As the Prayer Book directs, the priest places hands on the bread and wine while repeating Jesus' words at the Last Supper. Often, the priest elevates the bread and wine at the end of the Great Thanksgiving. Members of the congregation may also cross themselves when the words of the prayer ask the Holy

Spirit to sanctify the gifts and to sanctify us. In all these ways we are reminded frequently that this is a drama in which we are involved.

Sursum Corda, Preface, and Sanctus lead into the longest prayer in the liturgy, the *Great Thanksgiving.* It has several distinct parts. First, we give God thanks (we bless God) for the gift of Jesus' life, death, and resurrection. Next, the prayer recalls what Jesus did at the Last Supper. Then we pray for God to send the Holy Spirit upon the gifts and upon the congregation so that they and we may be transformed by the Spirit's presence. In the Middle Ages, Christians often argued about exactly how the bread and wine become the body and blood of Christ. It might be interesting to know that, but it is somewhat like worrying about how the members of the congregation came to be present at the service. Some probably walked, while others came by car. Perhaps some came by boat, helicopter, or on roller blades. It may be interesting to know that also, but it makes no difference to the service. If the people are present, no matter how they got there, the service can go on. Likewise, if Jesus is present in the bread and wine, then, no matter how it comes about, we can be given the gift of life. Episcopalians are, on the whole, more interested in facts than theories. It has been our tradition simply to speak of the *Real Presence,* and we are free to explain that presence in whatever terms make sense to us. However interesting theological speculation may be to theologians, it is very secondary to the fact that God feeds and nourishes us through the bread and wine that we have offered. That is why we come.

It is not surprising that medieval clergy fell into the habit of drawing attention to the words Jesus spoke at the Last Supper, and even thinking of them as a kind of formula of consecration. It is a moment of solemn mystery, and Jesus' own words seem to stand out. The Reformers also emphasized these words. Both Lutheran and Anglican liturgies specified that the bread and wine should be held up for all to see, and that people come to communion immediately after those words were spoken. Even though modern liturgical scholars agree that it is the entire prayer through which the bread and wine are transformed, the Prayer Book still directs that the priest lay a hand on the bread and the wine or to hold it as Jesus' words are repeated. Following the medieval tradition, in some churches the bread and wine are held up at this point. Sometimes a deacon or an acolyte rings a bell to call attention to the moment. These customs, and many others, vary widely in the Episcopal Church, as we have already noted.

We have already described the liturgy as being very much like a sacred dance with symbolic movements. These gestures are often very evident during the prayer of consecration. Many clergy, for example, hold their hands apart as they say, "The Lord be with you," raise them as they say, "Lift up your hearts," and then extend them again as they move into the main body of the prayer. Whether the priest's hands are held up or out, the intention is to indicate an attitude of prayerful expectancy; we come as suppliants before God and hold out our hands to receive holy gifts. The priest traditionally does this on behalf of the congregation, but it has become common in recent years to see members of the congregation hold up their hands in prayer as well, and even while singing a hymn. Moving, that instinctive need to involve our bodies in our worship, is characteristic of worship in the Episcopal Church.

The Prayer Book offers four prayers for the Great Thanksgiving in Rite II, and two in Rite I. Most congregations use one of the prayers most of the year but switch to others for special times or seasons. The variety "keeps us awake" or helps us to see different aspects of meaning. Too much variety, however, is confusing, and keeps us from moving beyond the surface of the words to the deepest levels of understanding. As with the prayers of intercession, the alternative prayers of consecration come from a variety of times and places. Although Prayer A is based on the traditional form in the Book of Common Prayer, and Prayer D is based on the Liturgy of St. Basil from the fourth century, it is also true that Prayer A includes the work of a twentieth-century Episcopalian and elements of it can be dated to the second century. Prayer D has been thoroughly rewritten by a modern committee of Anglican, Roman Catholic, and Protestant scholars. All of these prayers are evidence that even committees can do good work; they bring together the insights and wisdom of Christians from every age and place. The alternative Eucharistic prayers can be found at the end of the service, between pages 340 and 343 in Rite I and between pages 367 and 376 for Rite II.

Aside from the sermon, the Great Thanksgiving is the longest time when we listen to one voice. The priest is always speaking for the congregation, but the congregation joins in a dialog at the beginning, an acclamation in the middle, and a vitally important *AMEN* at the end. That last word is capitalized in the Prayer Book to emphasize its importance. This is our prayer, and it needs our endorsement. Often the bread and wine are held up together at this point in the service to allow the congregation to say the *AMEN* not simply to the prayer, but to the consecrated bread and wine through which Christ is coming to us.

After the *AMEN,* we join in saying the Lord's Prayer, without which no service is complete.

### THE BREAKING OF THE BREAD

The third action of the Eucharist is the *Breaking of the Bread.* This is a simple, practical action. Jesus broke bread at the Last Supper in order to distribute it to the disciples, just as

we break bread today to share it. In the Middle Ages the custom grew up of simplifying things by replacing the loaf of
bread with many small white discs, one for each communicant. These communion wafers were more convenient for the
priest but less symbolic than a whole loaf of bread broken to be
shared. It is still the custom in many churches to use individual
wafers, but the practice seems to be dying out. Pita bread, a flat
bread probably more like what was actually used at the Last
Supper, is commonly used today in many places, as well as
larger loaves of bread.

Whatever the parish custom may be, the priest will hold up
the loaf or a wafer and break it, saying words from St. Paul's
First Epistle to the Corinthians: "Christ our Passover is sacri-
ficed for us" (1 Corinthians 5:7; Prayer Book, 337 and 364)
The congregation responds with the next phrase from the
same passage: "Therefore let us keep the feast." Throughout
the rest of the year, except during Lent, the priest and congregation may add, "Alleluia," as at Easter. Another anthem,
called the *Agnus Dei* (Lamb of God) is also frequently said or
sung during or after the breaking of the bread. When John the
Baptist first announced the coming of the Messiah by pointing
to Christ, he said, "Here is the Lamb of God who takes away
the sin of the world!"(John 1:29) The anthem based on those
words serves the same purpose today in announcing the coming
of Christ to us.

In the earliest days of the church, the "breaking of bread"
was such a dramatic event that the whole service was referred
to by that name (cf. Acts 2:42, 46) It became the most significant ceremony for remembering Christ, and its importance
was evident from the very beginning. It was, as we have said,
on the evening of Easter Day that two disciples recognized the
Risen Christ when he broke bread with them. This action,
repeated by the disciples, not only functioned as a sign of his

presence but, for Christians, came to represent the breaking of Christ's body on the cross for our sake. It is because his body was broken that we are not only fed by it, but also made members of that body. The holding up and breaking of the bread may be a simple action, quickly performed, but it holds enormous significance. One of the anthems sometimes used at this point in the service says, "Be known to us, Lord Jesus, in the breaking of the bread."

## COMMUNION

The breaking of the bread is followed immediately by the fourth action of the Eucharist, the sharing of *communion.* The most common practice in the Episcopal Church is for members to come forward to kneel at an altar rail, symbolizing the family of God gathered in unity around God's table. In recent years, however, especially at large services, it has become increasingly common to have clergy and assistants stand at the head of the aisle or at other convenient places in the church so that those coming to communion can come in a line and receive the bread and wine while standing. Years ago, when this practice was used for the first time in a certain church, a woman complained to the rector that she had felt "like a beggar in a bread line." "What's wrong with that?" asked the rector. Most of us forget that each breath we take is a gift and that we have no claim on God's gifts except through God's mercy. We are indeed beggars in a bread line, no matter how large our bank accounts, and the bread we are given here nourishes us far better than the meals provided for us elsewhere, whether it be at a soup kitchen, our home, or the finest restaurant.

The first Christians are most likely to have received communion while reclining at a table, as the disciples would have done at the Last Supper. Anglicans attempted to imitate that practice after the Reformation by coming forward to kneel

around an altar placed lengthwise in the choir. The Invitation
in the Rite I service to "draw near with faith" is a relic of the
days when those intending to receive communion would
respond by moving forward into the choir and kneeling
around the altar for the remainder of the service. Eventually it
became customary to come forward only at communion time
and then not to the altar itself, but to an altar rail across the
chancel. Now customs are changing again, and there is no single, proper way to come to this central moment in the service
and in our lives. It is a solemn but joyful moment. It is a cor-
porate action, but it has enormous personal significance. It is
an age-old, universal action, shaped by local customs and preferences, the layout of the church, and other practical consider-
ations.

If the congregation is more than a handful at a weekday service, ushers usually regulate the flow of communicants to the
altar. This is simply a convenience, so that the whole congregation doesn't line up at one time and spend a long time standing
in the aisles. Most congregations follow a regular procedure for
coming to the altar and returning to the pews. The ushers usually begin at the front and work back. Communicants go forward through the center aisle and then, if the layout of the
church permits, return down side aisles to get back to their
seats. For newcomers, it will be a case of "follow the leader"
until they understand the local custom.

How do we receive communion? Customs vary from parish
to parish and within each parish as well, influenced by individual upbringing, customs, and personal preferences. Most clergy
and lay assistants are quite prepared to give communion to
people in several ways. The most traditional method is for
communicants to hold up both hands with the right hand
open over the left, because the right hand is the traditional
place of honor. The priest places the bread on the upper hand

and the communicant carries it to the mouth with both hands. It is helpful to the priest if the hands are open flat, not cupped, so that the bread can be placed there easily. The communicant then waits for the priest or an assistant to come with the chalice and takes the bottom of the chalice to guide the cup to the lips. Some, however, keep the bread, waiting for the wine. They then take the bread in their fingers, dip an edge lightly in the wine and place it in their mouths. In some parishes, the priest or assistant takes the bread, dips it, and places it on the communicant's tongue. Communicants who have been brought up in the Roman Catholic tradition, where they learned to receive the bread on their tongues, may prefer to continue to do so. Finally, some communicants are recovering alcoholics who prefer not to receive the wine at all. They may fold their arms to indicate to the chalice administrator that they will not receive, or they may simply leave the rail after receiving the bread.

A word about children may be in order. There was a time when no one was admitted to communion in the Episcopal Church except those who were confirmed "or ready and desirous to be confirmed." Nowadays that custom seems inconsistent with the emphasis on baptism as the sacrament that conveys full membership in the church (cf. Prayer Book, 298). As a result, children may now be admitted to communion and, in many parishes, even infants in arms may be given a taste of the bread and wine. Some parishes also have a procedure for giving children instruction before admitting them to communion, while at others some clergy and parents still hold to the older pattern of confirmation before first communion. Children—and adults—who for whatever reason are not prepared to receive communion may always come to the altar, fold their arms across their chests, and receive a blessing from the priest.

The various ways of receiving communion are partly a
result of a modern fear of germs, but germs expire very quickly
on a gold or silver surface washed with the alcohol and tannins
in the wine. People are far likelier to come into contact with
germs in the handshakes of the Peace or during the coffee hour
after the service. The clergy, who are always the last to drink
from the cup since they ordinarily consume what is left, are no
more prone to diseases than anyone else. During an epidemic,
or when someone has a raging cold, it may be wise to avoid
drinking from the common cup, but under most circumstances
it is probably less hazardous to our health than shaking hands.

What is it we receive? Perhaps it is a small wafer of unleav-
ened bread, or perhaps it is a piece of pita bread or a larger loaf,
but the gift we receive is life, the life of Christ poured into our
lives. It is *communion,* coming-into-union with God in Christ.
Our lives are joined with the life at the center of the universe
through which all life was created and in which all life exists. It
is also a coming-into-union with the church here on earth and
above. It is a moment when time and space cease to exist, and
we know that unity that is the goal of all our longing.

When the last communicant has left the altar rail, the
priest and assistants spend a few minutes cleansing the communion vessels. The bread and wine will not be blessed again;
they may be reverently consumed at that point or after the
service. They may also be reserved for use during the week, to
take to those who are too ill to be with the community. You
may notice a candle burning above the altar, off to one side,
or in a chapel to indicate that the sacrament is present there.
Many parishes have a system for taking communion immediately to those who are too weak to attend, whether they are at
home, in the hospital, or in a nursing home. People called *Lay
Eucharistic Ministers* may be sent from the altar immediately

after communion to carry the sacrament to these others. Often, too, a priest or deacon may take the Sacrament to such members later in the week.

## SENT ON MISSION

For many centuries before the Reformation, (and many centuries afterwards in the Roman Catholic Church, which continued to pray in Latin) the Eucharist ended with the words, *Ite, missa est,* sometimes translated, "Go, you are sent," and the whole service became known as the *missa* or *mass* because of those final words.

Why should the whole service take its name from the final words? Because the whole service has been leading up to these words and what will come afterwards. The congregation does not simply leave; it is sent forth into the world with a mission. The word *missa* is also directly connected to the modern English word *mission,* and those who have worshiped God come away from that worship with a mission to carry out: to serve and bear witness. Each individual finds unique opportunities to do that in ways as different as the members themselves. To return to St. Paul's analogy, some of us are hands and some are feet, while others are mouths and eyes and ears. Some of us serve God best by loving our immediate family, friends, and business associates, working to understand their needs, and helping them toward their goals. Many of us take on particular assignments by serving on vestries and altar guilds, volunteering in soup kitchens, teaching church school, or helping with routine building maintenance. Some bear witness to God's love by talking with newcomers at the coffer hour, visiting the sick or shut-in, or helping maintain the church web site. Still others take up full-time mission work, whether short term or long term. There is a need for people with special skills as teachers and medical personnel in many places in this country and overseas, and the national church office can help match skills with needs. Even those who are confined to a nursing home or hospital bed can take part in the church's mission by praying for those more actively engaged. No one can say, "The church has no need of me." The Prayer Book provides a choice of three dismissal sentences, but the one most often used is, "Go in peace to love and serve the Lord." That is the job description for those who are going out on mission. In parishes where a deacon is part of the ordained ministry team, it is the deacon who says these words. We mentioned earlier in this book the deacon's role in servant ministry. It is appropriate, therefore, for the deacon to say these words, calling on the whole membership of the church to join in the ministry of service to the world.

Unfortunately, it is easy to lose sight of the meaning of the dismissal in the confusion of the ending of the service. Some people value a brief prayer and time of silence so they stay after the service for a few moments. Though it would be logical to follow the words of dismissal by opening the door and standing back as people stream out on mission, few churches do so. It sometimes seems as if those who plan the service are reluctant to see it end or to let people go out to do what they are sent to do. Christians have always had a certain quite understandable reluctance to go from that place where they have had such joy and peace, and the instinct to add prayers and blessings and hymns is very natural. All that is really needed, however, is the dismissal, the marching order. In the days before the Reformation, when people seldom received communion, a blessing by the priest or bishop was added to the end of the service so they would at least have received something. Those who have received communion need no further blessing, but old habits die hard, and often the blessing is still added. Often, too, there is a choir that needs to march out. Frequently the dismissal is said, people are directed to leave, and then a hymn begins that prevents them from leaving. It's all a little odd! But keep your eye on the ball: the dismissal is the critical element, and in many churches it really is the last word. The choir marches out, the deacon or priest says, "Go," and people get up and go out to serve God in the world around them. Why, after all, did we come in, except to get the strength to go out and do the work God has given us to do?

## QUESTIONS FOR FURTHER
## THOUGHT AND DISCUSSION

1. The author suggests that because so many things are happening simultaneously during the Offertory that it's easy to "miss the point" by overlooking the central meaning. Do you find this to be true? What can you do to bring the true purpose of the Offertory into focus?

2. What does the term *Real Presence,* as it relates to the Eucharist, mean to you?

3. What does the breaking of the bread represent? What else?

4. How do most people receive communion in your church? Does that method suit you, or do you prefer some other way? Why?

5. What are your views on the practice of allowing children to receive communion before they have been confirmed?

6. Before reading this chapter, did you know where the term *mass* came from? How will you respond to those final words, "Go, you are sent"?

# In Conclusion

In rather small print on one of the last pages of the Book of Common Prayer (864ff.) is a document called The Creed of Saint Athanasius. It is very long and strangely worded, but it begins with a very fundamental declaration: that to be saved we must "hold the Catholic Faith . . . and the Catholic Faith is this, That we worship one God in Trinity, and Trinity in unity." At the heart of the Christian faith is the establishment of a relationship between human beings and God through worship.

Who would have believed that to be possible? Any introductory course in science will provide you with information beyond your imagination: that the universe is fifteen billion years old, that it would take four years at the speed of light to reach the nearest star, that the universe is expanding at enormous speed, and that each particle of matter is related to every other particle by gravitational, electro-magnetic, and nuclear forces so that particles at opposite ends of the universe move in partnership. Christians believe that the Creator of this unimaginable universe, in which we are just transitory specks, created us out of love, and for the sake of that relationship became flesh in Jesus of Nazareth. If we are not overawed by our knowledge of the universe, we can hardly help being overawed by the knowledge of the Creator's love.

Therefore, we worship. There is nothing God needs that we might offer. There is nothing we can do to deserve such a relationship. But we can praise God and worship. Christians are called to do more than worship, of course. There is a world that needs our witness. We have good news to tell and neighbors everywhere who need our help. But worship is where the Christian life begins. It is through worship that we are united with God and strengthened to bear witness and serve. That is why, for nearly five hundred years, Anglicans have found their unity and strength in a Book of Common Prayer and a tradition of worship. This book may help the reader to understand that tradition and enter into it more fully. If it serves that purpose well, it will open up a way of life that has eternal value.

## MEET THE AUTHOR:
## CHRISTOPHER L. WEBBER

 Christopher L. Webber grew up in the Episcopal Church, in a very small parish in upstate New York. After graduating from Princeton University, he attended the General Theological Seminary in New York City, and went on to serve as a parish priest in places as varied as Brooklyn, Tokyo, and the rural northwestern corner of Connecticut.

With his move to Connecticut in 1994, Father Webber's interest in writing—which had already produced several books —developed into a career. *Welcome to Sunday* is the author's sixteenth book. Included in Father Webber's writing are several volumes of poetry and two collections of hymns that paraphrase the psalms and other biblical passages. Father Webber's other books are on church-related themes, and they include *Welcome to the Episcopal Church, The Art of the Homily,* and *The User's Guide to the Holy Eucharist. Praise the Lord, My Soul,* a beautifully illustrated version of Psalm 104 for children, was published by Morehouse in 2002.

In his spare time, Father Webber enjoys the challenges of country living: caring for a large garden and orchard, making a small supply of maple syrup each spring, and cutting and splitting firewood.

Father Webber has been married for more than forty years to Margaret Elisabeth Rose Webber, a travel consultant who has organized  pilgrimages that the couple has led to Israel, Scotland, and England. Travel is a major interest; recent trips have taken them to Australia, New Zealand, Fiji, and Canada.

The Webbers have four children and three  grandchildren.

## ALSO BY CHRISTOPHER L. WEBBER

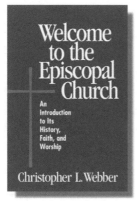

**An**
**Introduction**
**to Its**
**History,**
**Faith, and**
**Worship**

Christopher L. Webber

ISBN 0-8192-1820-0

**Welcome to the Episcopal Church**
An Introduction to Its History, Faith, and Worship

Written in accessible language in a conversational tone, this introduction to the Episcopal Church is the ideal resource for adult parish study, newcomers, and other interested individuals. From an Episcopal perspective, the author explores Episcopal history, worship, beliefs, spiritual life, organization, mission and outreach, and the way we read and understand the Bible. Study questions accompany each chapter.

*Welcome to the Episcopal Church* "makes clear that the worship of God is the most important thing that can be said about us, and that worship is the source for everything else in our life together—our commitment to justice for all people, our mission to those who do not yet know Jesus Christ as their Lord and Savior, and how we should live out our lives in this very complex world." —from the Foreword by the Most Reverend Frank T. Griswold III, Presiding Bishop and Primate

Available from Morehouse Publishing
800-877-0012
www.morehousepublishing.com

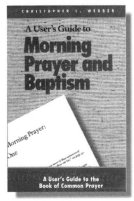

ISBN 0-8192-1696-8

## A User's Guide to Morning Prayer and Baptism

Become a full partner in the worship services of the Episcopal Church by using this guide, which illuminates the theology, history, and practical concerns of the liturgy. Developed specifically to address the needs of inquirers and others not familiar with The Book of Common Prayer, this volume provides a running commentary on two of the major services. It includes the complete text of Morning Prayer and Baptism from The Book of Common Prayer, a glossary, and lists of books for further reading.

"The only way you can really get to know God is through prayer," says author Christopher L. Webber, "and the Prayer Book sets out a pattern that has been used by saints and sinners for centuries. No other book will give you as much help in building your faith. This guide will get you started on understanding that book."